CAPITAL
A Moral Instrument?

With Foreword by Raymond Johnstone, CBE

Published on behalf of
THE CENTRE FOR THEOLOGY AND PUBLIC ISSUES
UNIVERSITY OF EDINBURGH
by SAINT ANDREW PRESS, EDINBURGH

First published in 1992 by SAINT ANDREW PRESS
121 George Street, Edinburgh EH2 4YN
on behalf of THE CENTRE FOR THEOLOGY AND PUBLIC ISSUES
UNIVERSITY OF EDINBURGH

ISBN 0 86153 149 3

British Library Cataloguing-in-Publication Data
    Centre for Theology and Public Issues
    Capital: a moral instrument?
    I. Title
    241.644

ISBN 0-86153-149-3

This book is set in 11/12 pt Times Roman.

*The Centre gratefully acknowledges
financial assistance from
The Drummond Trust, 3 Pitt Street, Stirling,
in the production of this book*

Contents

Foreword   vii
Mr Raymond Johnstone, CBE
Chairman of Scottish Financial Enterprise

Introduction   ix
Members of Working Group on Finance and Ethics   xi

1 An Ethical Concern   1
2 Wealth Creation   9
3 Credit   16
4 The Market   26
5 The Market-place and the Responsible Investor   37
6 Christians in the Financial World Today   46

Appendices

1 Adam Smith: Ethics and Self-interest   55
2 Wealth and Riches — Ethics and Morality   57
3 Is there a Duty of Self-fulfilment?   62
4 Bank Secrecy and Money Laundering   65
5 Ethical Investment   68
6 Credit Unions   72
7 Memorandum submitted to the Independent
   Inquiry into Corporate Takeovers in the United
   Kingdom, April 1990   74

Foreword

I am particularly pleased to have the opportunity to write a Foreword for this discussion of finance and ethics by the University of Edinburgh's Centre for Theology and Public Issues.

Scotland has shown throughout its history an ability to think clearly about the issues involved in commercial life and in banking and finance, in a way that has combined practical business considerations with ethical responsibility. The name of Adam Smith leaps to mind with his *The Wealth of Nations* and *The Theory of Moral Sentiments*.

We have been through a time when legislation and increasing control perhaps stultified initiative; this was followed by a decade in which market liberalisation will have been perceived by many as having allowed greed to get the upper hand in the natural interplay of fear and greed which so dominates free markets. Over the same period the public has developed a much closer interest in the ethical considerations concerning markets, and mechanisms have been put in place for the self-regulation of financial businesses. What better moment could there be to have an objective assessment of the issues?

As one of the Consultants to the project I was invited to some discussion meetings. Discussion of ethical standards using as a yardstick Christian teaching shows up how little the standards of the world change over time, and spotlights the difference in concept between wealth creation and wealth accumulation. I found the clarity of thought of participants — who were mostly not involved in the daily round of financial decision-taking — to be very refreshing on the basic issues, just as are the papers reproduced in this volume.

The probity of financial advisers is a key to the regard in which they are held. It is to me very positive that these papers should come from such an appropriate Scottish group, and I am sure they will clear the minds of many people both within the financial sector and outside it. I very much welcome this publication.

MR RAYMOND JOHNSTONE, CBE
Chairman of Scottish Financial Enterprise

Introduction

This publication is the result of a two-year study by a group of financial practitioners and theologians working under the sponsorship of the University of Edinburgh's Centre for Theology and Public Issues. The group met once per month over two years and twice spent the best part of a day in conference.

As was to be expected, in the initial stages the discussion ranged widely over the many subjects which might be included under the heading of "finance and ethics". About the beginning of the second year, however, in order to give some focus to the discussions, the six subjects included here were chosen and worked on for the remainder of the contracted period.

Some members and consultants were invited to provide additional comments filling out some of the points mentioned in the main report; these appear as appendices. The Group's submission to the Independent Inquiry into Mergers and Takeovers has also been included as an illustration of the practical application of ethics to current problems.

It is with some surprise, and it cannot be without significance, that a group whose members have such diverse backgrounds and differing interests has yet been able to discover much common ground on issues which tend to divide. Our aim was to "seek enlightenment" and this we believe we have achieved to a considerable extent. Our hope is that we may share this with a wider audience through this publication.

We recognise, of course, that this is only part of an ongoing debate and we are encouraged by the fact that ethical issues are being given much more prominence in current thinking about financial practices and structures for the future. We ourselves intend to continue to promote such thinking in various settings and within a variety of groupings.

We invite anyone who would be interested in taking part to contact us at the Centre in Edinburgh.

Finally, we are grateful to Mr Raymond Johnstone, CBE, one of our most helpful Consultants, and a greatly respected figure in the Scottish financial community, for agreeing to provide a Foreword commending this venture.

REVD GEORGE WILKIE
Chairman

Members of Working Group on Finance and Ethics

Robin J Angus
Director, County Natwest Woodmac

David Berridge
Chief Executive, Scottish Equitable Assurance Society

Robert Dalgleish
MSF Trade Union

Brian Dick
Financial Director, Noble Grossart PLC

Revd Ronald Ferguson
Minister, St Magnus Cathedral, Kirkwall, Orkney

James G S Gammell
Ex-Chairman, Ivory and Sime PLC

George Harte
Lecturer, Accounting and Business Methods, Edinburgh University

Alan Macfarlane
Director, Ivory and Sime PLC

David MacLeod
Divinity Student, ex-Citibank

Dr Charles W Munn
Chief Executive, Chartered Institute of Bankers of Scotland

Revd Donald Ross
Industrial Mission Organiser, Church of Scotland

Dr Andrew Russell
Ex-Treasurer, Bank of Scotland

Joanna K Storrar
Ex-Investment Manager, New York

Very Revd Professor James A Whyte
Emeritus Professor, Practical Theology and Christian Ethics, St Andrews University

Revd George Wilkie
Associate Director, Centre for Theology and Public Issues, Edinburgh University (Chairman of Working Group)

1

An Ethical Concern

Financial surplus

One of the many discontinuities between our own and previous ages is the fact that today many ordinary people (in the West at least) have moved beyond subsistence living to a standard of living which provides them with an increasing financial surplus which can be used to generate further wealth. The acquisition and increase of such a surplus has become for many a central concern of life, so much so that commentators like Anthony Sampson have described it as the "New Religion" and dubbed the great Stock Exchange buildings as the "cathedrals" of our day, where the great god "Money" receives the adoration of his worshippers.

To judge from the increased attention given to financial matters in the popular press and in the media generally, there is widespread interest in this area of life among the general public. Finance is an area in which many people's fathers and grandfathers would never have expected to be involved — indeed, they might have been highly critical of those who dealt in the buying and selling of shares. But the children of this age have an increasing stake in the activities of the financial community and have embraced its spirit and practices without much apparent concern over the ethical problems which worried their forefathers. Today's "ethical" concerns are more likely to be with the functioning of the market than with the fundamental legitimacy of the system itself.

There has, of course, been considerable governmental support over the past decade for the idea of "popular capitalism". There is an attractiveness about getting involved in the ownership of industry and in the economic future of your country and many have taken up the challenge with gusto. At the same time, financial institutions have developed new structures and tailored their wares for the new breed of customer, with the object of making investment simpler and of spreading ever wider the ownership of capital. Through unit trusts, life assurance, pension funds, investment trusts and various forms of banking, an increasing number of people in this country now have a stake in what happens in the financial world.

Global market

All this is happening while we are increasingly becoming members of "one world". Propelled by advances in information technology, there has been a great push towards a 24-hour global market, with money rushing round the world in seconds and frenzied dealers moving in and out of shares scores of times a year. This makes what is happening so much more complex and the risk of confusion and failure that much greater.

This trend also renders transactions much more impersonal. People need no longer meet to exchange. Business can be done "over the wire". The market takes on a life of its own and becomes less related to the real world of industry and commerce which it is supposed to support. This is one of the issues which gives rise to anxiety about the financial structures today. An American commentator has said: "In the 80s you don't have to be productive to make money." And it has been calculated that most American billionaires did not make their money by what would generally be regarded as productive work, as their counterparts in previous generations had done.

Moreover, where people from different cultures begin to trade in the same global market, there is bound to be uncertainty about standards and a danger that the lowest common denominator will prevail. The problem of ethics in a pluralist society is one which a uniting world has to face on many fronts, not least in relation to the degree to which the values and financial practices of different cultures are compatible.

Another consequence of becoming one world is that people in the less favoured parts of the world (many of whom still live in a subsistence economy) now have their expectations raised. Bombarded by images of the consumerist West, it no longer seems to the ordinary person in these countries that they need remain in their present state. Rather, they feel that it is the right of every one of earth's citizens to gain the standard of life now enjoyed by most people in the West.

Uneasiness

While many of these recent developments are inevitable, and are indeed to be welcomed for enhancing the standard of living of a great many people, there is also a certain uneasiness, both among those directly involved and among the public at large, about some aspects of the growing financial sector. There are, of course, many who operate within this sector who see their work in terms of a service both for clients and for industry and commerce. But even amongst the strongest supporters of our present highly developed market economy, there is concern about the spirit which now seems to permeate much of its life and activity. Excessive greed, aggression, acquisitiveness and a lack of concern for those affected by market activity seem to be characteristics increasingly in evidence in financial dealings. The scandals which emerged from the City and Wall Street during the 1980s highlighted these aspects of today's markets.

If "righteousness exalteth a nation" (Proverbs 14:34) it cannot be good for any society to have one of its central and most pervasive institutions motivated in this way. And it is such an attitude in high places that is more likely to trickle down to the rest of society than the financial benefit which is expected and promised. If, as it is claimed, a certain structure of welfare benefits has created a spirit of dependency in one sector of society, so a structure which enshrines naked avarice will produce in another sector a spirit of self-centred individualism which is ultimately anarchic and destructive of true community.

Ethical questions

In general, then, there is a widespread feeling that certain sectors of the financial community have broken loose from the constraints of the past and from the values of a society which did not have the mak ng of money out of money as its number one priority. Most of us are involved in this financial world either as practitioners or as beneficiaries. And many of us are troubled by doubts about the ethics of it all — and about the inevitable outcome if the ethical issues are not faced.

The financial world is not an autonomous realm, operating according to its own laws. Because financial enterprise is a human activity, ethical issues are involved. And although Christians have no monopoly of the understanding of financial ethics, they have a responsibility to see that the pertinent issues are raised.

Aims of the working group

It was against this background that a Working Group was set up within the University of Edinburgh's Centre for Theology and Public Issues composed of financial practitioners and theologians, with the following aims:

> To examine areas of life in which finance is involved and where ethical issues arise and to seek theological and biblical references to bring enlightenment and guidance both for those involved and for society as a whole.

Two preliminary points had to be faced. Firstly, what do we mean by ethics? And secondly, since the ethics we are concerned about are explicitly Christian, how do we see the Bible as a source of ethical insight?

What do we mean by ethics?

When people talk about ethics they tend to think about right and wrong as clear opposites which can be stated in principle and related to any situation. In fact, ethical thinking has used a much wider range of concepts, such as value, goodness, virtue and happiness in thinking about human attitudes and human behaviour. But the popular demand for ethics is a demand for a clear statement of right and wrong.

When Christians take this attitude, they frequently look to the Bible for a set of absolute rules which will immediately give answers to the question of what is right and what is wrong, and they expect the Church to formulate these for them. The attempt to do this leads to a legalistic attitude to human life, which is a denial of personal responsibility. Far from providing clarity, this leads to constant modification, qualification and argument regarding insignificant details (straining gnats and swallowing camels) while it also encourages a devious search for ways of obeying the letter of the law while ignoring its spirit.

Jesus, who saw this tendency in the Pharisees, provided a new basis for ethical judgements. This was not a set of rules to be applied unthinkingly, but rather glimpses of life in God's Kingdom, which we should aspire to. His task was not to give easy answers, but to encourage men and women to work things out for themselves in accordance with what they knew of God's will. Such a wider view of ethics means for us that we are not just dealing with the rightness or wrongness of particular actions, but with the whole context of structures, working practices and outcomes involving both individuals and institutions in our world today.

Jesus was also aware that our actions are not necessarily all good or all bad. They are often a mixture of good and bad and don't respond to the "absolute rule" approach. His parable of the wheat and the tares (Matthew 13:15) in which the farmer restrained his men from pulling up the tares in case they pulled up the wheat as well, suggests that we have to recognise that there is imperfection in many if not all of our actions. But the inevitable presence of evil should not mean that we stop trying to do good. We have to learn to live with our failures and not be paralysed into inaction for fear that we make a mistake. Christians live by God's forgiveness and not by their own rightness.

In adopting this approach, Jesus is not trying to make things easier for Christians by removing hard and fast rules. He is really asking for a bigger and more comprehensive form of goodness. With relation to financial life this means that we must not only be looking for rights and wrongs, but for whatever promotes a healthy society, which is to be supported, and whatever destroys human community, which is to be opposed.

The Bible as a source of ethical insights

In our use of the Bible as a source of ethical insights we are faced with the question: "Can a book — the Bible — written against the background of a primitive agrarian society provide any insights for the highly complex technological society of today?''

If the Bible is to be of use to us we must recognise it for what it is. We persist in wanting "biblical answers" — preferably with proof texts. But there are no "biblical answers" — or rather, there are often many, and they may be answers to different questions in different circumstances. We will only hear what the Bible says if we treat it with proper respect. This means acknowledging differences within the biblical literature and between the biblical world and our own.

The Decalogue (Ten Commandments), for instance, is not a basis for personal morality. It is a code for a community, an essential basis for a social ethic. It lays down boundaries, (*eg* respect for human life, respect for property, respect for family, respect for truth), expressing a strong sense of national community. The Prophets also voice this concern for the welfare and well-being of all in the city, expressing anger at cruelty, callousness and lack of brotherhood.

Admittedly, in the Old Testament there is savagery, xenophobia, harsh social legislation and ritualism, but beneath it all is a broad human concern — for the poor, for strangers, for the unfortunate. Of course, the Old Testament is "this worldly" in its outlook and proclaims no belief in an afterlife. But it demonstrates clearly that corruption destroys a society.

In the New Testament, Christians are in a different situation from that of the Jews in the Old Testament. The Jews were always a nation, even when in exile, even when subjugated. Christians were a minority, of many nations, in many nations, a sect in a pagan society with no responsibility for rule or for making laws. In the Epistles we find ethics for a community liberated by the Gospel. The attitudes encouraged are those which build up the Christian community. Those which are outlawed are those which disrupt and destroy community (*cf* Galatians 5:19–22). These pointers to good living are not a code of law, and they are not exhaustive. The Epistles also contain advice to the Christian communities not to exercise their liberty in a way that would give offence to their neighbours or cause needless scandal. Such advice clearly belongs within its own social context, though the principles behind it may be of abiding value.

The Sermon on the Mount has often been regarded as the new Law, and perhaps Matthew intends us to see it as such. Nevertheless, attempts to treat it as law are self-defeating, and sometimes morally objectionable (*eg* if I give to everyone who asks and leave my family to starve). It is perhaps better to see the precepts of Jesus as an attack on the *way* of law, with its essentially limited responsibility. (So that one can say: "I have done so much. I have kept the law.") The Sermon, rather, presents in vivid and highly selective pictures a glimpse of love's unlimited responsibility, an attitude of openness and availability to the other. It is an ideal which always judges our limited responses, but it should not prevent us acting with prudence and with wisdom in determining what, in our situations, our responses should be.

In the parables Jesus tells stories of everyday life. Some evoke common domestic scenes, like the story of the woman sweeping the room to find the coin she has lost (Luke 15:9); some are more fanciful, like the story of the king who goes on a long journey, leaving his servants in charge of his property (Matthew 21:34). The stories were often puzzling, in order to make people think. Sometimes they ended in a question: "Which of the two ...?" Sometimes they were prefaced by the words: "The Kingdom of Heaven is like ..." One might say that they show us the nature of the Kingdom and the surprising generosity and equally surprising judgement of God. It is on the basis of such insights that we have to attempt an ethical response to the situations we face in the world of our day.

The values of the Kingdom

Many Christians today affirm strongly that this is God's world; their hope is that, in the words of the ancient prayer, "The Kingdoms of the world shall become the Kingdom of our God and of His Christ." How this is to be understood or realised is the problem. Jesus didn't seem to think of two separate spheres, sacred and profane, religious and secular, spiritual and material, but of the world and the life within it as being God's, to be seen in the light of his purposes. The Kingdom of God is not a purely spiritual sphere, unrelated to the life of this world. Nor is it a blueprint, a new Law for this world, which can be imposed on it by reform or revolution or even by the power of the Church. The world has to be seen in the light of the Kingdom which is always over it, to judge and to beckon.

The question for us is: "Can the values of the Kingdom interpenetrate — in any degree — our worlds of business and finance?"

And perhaps we might also ask: "Have they done so already?"

2
Wealth Creation

The Church's attitude

The Church is accused of being unrealistic in its opposition to wealth creation and wealth creators. Lord Hailsham is reported to have said: "We can do with fewer clerics who decry wealth creation as mere greed ... We must encourage the creation of wealth as a socially responsible activity."

The Church is also accused of talking a lot about the distribution of wealth without recognising the need to create it. We should learn, it is said, from the failure of the East European countries to create wealth, a failure which has meant that they have had little to distribute. Wealth creation has to be a priority.

The Church is also accused of being hypocritical about wealth creators. Church leaders are frequently heard criticising the activities of those who are successful in business, but have no hesitation about appealing to them for financial help.

The popular view

Those who emphasise the importance of wealth creation usually measure it in terms of financial success. Not only must we give it priority, they say, but we must give individuals the freedom and the encouragement to create wealth (for themselves) with as few restrictions as possible. Our salvation lies with an "enterprise culture" which puts the emphasis on growth and whose future depends on risk-taking (and hard-working) entrepreneurs ever probing new areas of growth and new ways of creating wealth for themselves and (through a "trickle-down effect") for others.

The traditional Christian attitude

The popular view seems to contrast with the traditional
Christian attitude to wealth. There is no mention of the importance of wealth creation in Jesus' description of the
Kingdom of God, though Jesus was not unaware of the existence of wealth creators in his day (see the parable of the
talents, Matthew 25:15). Rather, there is a tendency in the
New Testament to play down the importance of wealth for
those who seek a full life: "A man's life consisteth not in
the abundance of the things he possesseth" (Luke 12:15);
"Life is more than meat, the body more than raiment"
(Matthew 6:25). There is also an emphasis on the dangers of
seeking or having riches because they so easily usurp the
place of God to the exclusion of the things that really bring
us life: "It will be hard for a rich man to get into the
Kingdom of God" (Matthew 19:23). We are assured that
God knows that we "have need of food and clothing"
(Matthew 6:32); and so we are told to "Take no anxious
thought for the morrow" (Matthew 6:34).

Jesus and wealth

For himself, Jesus obviously did not lay great store on
the accumulation of wealth. Indeed, in the Beatitudes he
claims the meek shall inherit the earth. During his working
days he was an ordinary village carpenter without any
obvious ambitions to expand his business! Then, as an
itinerant preacher, he had "nowhere to lay his head".
Like his Church, however, he was not unwilling to accept —
and indeed to request — an invitation to a rich man's
table.

In another sense, of course, Jesus has given us a perfect
example of true wealth creation. As a carpenter he took the
raw materials (wood) and by his skill and labour fashioned
them into tables and chairs and yokes and ploughs for the
benefit of mankind (and animal kind). Here, as everywhere
else, he was fulfilling God's purpose for man, and no doubt
it brings joy to the heart of God when men and women are
engaged in true wealth creation. The sad fact is that in our
society wealth creation is too often equated with wealth
accumulation, about which Jesus had many harsh things to
say.

Basic difference

An important factor which has to be taken into consideration when we think about wealth creation is the basic difference between the society of the first century and that of our own time. The society in which Jesus spoke was an economically *static* society in which, although there were a few rich people, most were living at or about subsistence level without any great expectation that things might change. Today we live in an economically *dynamic* society shaped by technologies which have opened up new possibilities for ordinary people and brought many blessings to everyone — health, housing, education, social services, food, travel, leisure, and so on. Was this in the intention of God? If so, we need to take the creation of wealth seriously.

Biblical witness

Is there anything in the biblical tradition which relates to the idea of wealth creation? It is part of the nature of creation that man has to use the earth's resources to support his life and to bring the joy which God intends from his gift of life. Words like "abundance", "increase" and "fruitfulness" are commonplace in the Bible. And there are many statements expressing the intention of God that mankind should enjoy the fruits of the earth, from the promise of a "land flowing with milk and honey" to Jesus' presence at the wedding feast. The earth's resources are not to be seen in puritanical terms as "forbidden fruit" but rather as evidence of God's generosity and of his desire that they should bring joy to human life.

The Bible also gives man a special place in creation. Whereas animals also enjoy the fruits of the earth, man is "made in the image of God" (Genesis 1:21) not just to consume but also to "tend and to keep" (Genesis 2:19) God's creation and to have part with God in his continuing act of creation. Christians dare to believe that man has a role as *steward of creation* — and this role is particularly vital given our situation today.

The way in which man uses God's creation to produce good things for life is through his work. Work is not just the hard labour of tilling and planting and harvesting, but involves the application of man's understanding, imagination, ingenuity, skill and invention to earth's resources in order to bring forth benefits for human life. In this sense wealth creation is clearly part of God's intention. As Professor Brian Griffiths says: "It stems from a fundamental human drive" (*The Creation of Wealth*, Hodder & Stoughton 1984). The Bible also reminds us of man's tendency to disobey God's command in work as in every other aspect of life, by wanting to do things his own way. When man begins to abuse this God-given ability to create things, pain, alienation and even disaster so often follow.

Enterprise and faith

God's will, then, is that man should have the opportunity through the use of his intelligence, ingenuity, strength *etc*, to "improve his lot", to enhance the quality of his own life and that of his family and of his neighbour. In such work man shares in God's work and is accountable for the use of God's creation.

Further, there seems to be a sense in which this challenge is issued to each individual. However important the sense of belonging in a community undoubtedly is, God calls each of us to a life of enterprise and faith in which we are to enter into life "in all its fulness", "working out our own salvation" — all in terms of the Kingdom of God. It also becomes much more vital that we work for a society in which every person has the opportunity to create wealth or to share in the creation of wealth, rather than being excluded from this essential part of what it is to be human.

Proper place

To acknowledge a biblical basis for wealth creation is not to say that it should be the central feature of human life, or that such was God's intention. "Man does not live by bread alone." Full barns satisfy animals but not human beings. To allow wealth creation legitimacy is not to endow it with authority. The message of the Bible is more often: "Love God and keep his commandments and you will be blessed." It is therefore necessary to keep wealth creation in its proper place in the Christian approach to life. We need to keep in mind all the New Testament warnings about being possessed by our possessions.

True wealth creation

It is also important to distinguish between the Bible's
approval of wealth creation in the terms described above
and the widespread notion that this approval means that we
should all strive to accumulate wealth. And it is here that the
central problem arises for Christians. What exactly can truly
be called wealth creation in all the activity that goes on
under that name today? The wealth creators who are held up
to us as the benefactors of our society are mainly people
who went about wealth creation single-mindedly and for
themselves. It is this activity which, it is maintained, should
be encouraged because it benefits society in general even
though the wealthy did not specifically intend it to do so —
and even if their genuine intention was to grab everything
for themselves.

It is the contrast between accepted Christian attitudes and
many of the methods of creating wealth today which poses
ethical questions for all of us and especially for those
involved daily in financial activities. It is right to recognise in
ourselves the God-given drive to improve our lot and to
enjoy the fruits of creation. Pushed to excess, however, and
allowed to become the dominant aim in life, this impulse
may inadvertently benefit some others but it will not bring
life to the wealth creator — and it may in fact bring disaster
to many others along the way. Some may choose to live this
way, but in Christian love we should not encourage that
particular form of wealth creation either for the individuals
concerned or as a foundation for the life of our society.
Some of the problems inherent in various methods of
creating wealth are examined in the following chapters on
credit, the market and the responsible investor.

The need for growth

We have already stated that one of the differences between
our society and that of Jesus' time is that we are an
economically dynamic society. Among other things this
means that ours is a society which takes continuing technological advancement for granted and is committed to
increased production and consumption, that is, to continual
growth. To stop the process of growth, it is said, would be
disastrous both for employment in this country and for world

trade and would inevitably result in a serious reduction in our standard of living. But can such a system be maintained in today's conditions? Indeed, *should* it be?

The challenge is twofold:

- *First*, we must examine our practices from an ecological point of view, giving consideration to the depletion of scarce resources, the pollution of air and water, the disposal of waste and the global climate changes that are now in evidence. Are we locked in to growth as a necessity of life regardless of the adverse effects it may have on human life today and tomorrow? Not to question this seems hardly to fulfil the stewardship role which Christians claim has been entrusted to mankind. As one leading Scottish investment manager has said: "We must leave the earth's resources in at least as good a state as we found them."
- *Second*, we must also ask: "Is there no room for 'contentment' in life?" The Tenth Commandment warns of the dangers of covetousness and yet is it not the logic of a growth-orientated economy that we must covet more and more of this world's goods? There seems to be a flaw in an economic system which makes this demand.

A more responsible way of talking about growth in the light of today's conditions may be in terms of the increase of the efficiency of production rather than an increase in its quantity, *ie* in terms of using renewable resources, recycling waste, reducing pollution and so on. This would certainly accord more closely with the concept of stewardship and the efforts of Christians should be bent to the task of promoting a wider acceptance of this approach. At the same time, the need for increased volume of production should not be overlooked — for the sake of the poor of the earth who seem to have been bypassed by the growth which has so much benefited us in the West.

Social responsibility

We must certainly take note of Lord Hailsham's plea that we encourage the creation of wealth as a socially responsible activity, but we must also challenge the sort of wealth creation which is socially irresponsible.

A lot of wealth creation has involved man using his God-given gifts of skill, intelligence, strength and enterprise for the good of all. But not all that goes by the name is wealth creation as God intended it. Christians individually and in groups need continually to promote those kinds of wealth creation which are "socially responsible" and to challenge those which are not.

God has given us the earth and its fruits for celebration. Only human selfishness can defeat his purposes. Christians come into this field not as kill-joys, but as promoters of a better way which will bring fulfilment for all.

3

Credit

Introduction

Money is a consumer's most basic tool. Borrowing
money is one crucial way for people to get the things
they need (or want) at the time they need them. They
satisfy current needs out of the expectation of future
income. It is clear that this creates both opportunity and
risk: the opportunity to meet current need now and the
risk that the expectation of future ability to pay may
be wrong (*Credit and Debt: the Consumer Interest*,
National Consumer Council).

Many voices are raised today about the spread of credit —
both individual and corporate. Many recognise its undoubted
benefits, such as assisting in the purchase of a home or
easing temporary financial problems. And it can also be
helpful — indeed life-saving — when misfortune hits a
family. But most people also acknowledge that there is a
growing number of "credit casualties".

A recent commentator has said: "Modern day society
is littered with spendthrifts – governments, companies,
institutions, individuals. Credit is their DRUG. Indeed a
spendthrift is a 'financial drug addict'."

It is certainly the case that the number of agencies from
which credit can be obtained has increased substantially in
recent years. There is a large array of providers, from banks
and building societies to retail stores. Indeed it has been
argued that some stores make more profit from their credit-
awarding activities than from retailing. No doubt in a time
of recession the problems associated with credit will be
heightened.

It is, however, easy to exaggerate the extent of these
problems. It should be remembered that consumer credit on
a large scale is a comparatively recent phenomenon, dating

from the late 1950s, and has undergone the most rapid growth in the 1980s. The main problems arise out of unforeseen circumstances, usually when people become ill or unemployed and their income stream is interrupted.

Another commentator recently said: "As society becomes richer, poverty and debt are rediscovered." While this is true, it is all too easy to confuse the debate on credit with the poverty debate, and although poor people are prone to difficulties with credit repayments, there is abundant evidence to show that more affluent people are also likely to have problems — hidden problems and pressures which fall short of default.

It is therefore a matter of concern that *credit is becoming institutionalised* in the lives of many people. Students, for example, are now expected — and encouraged — to take out loans to pay for their studies. Clearly, there may be longer-term benefits for the students, but the question should at least be raised as to whether this is the best method of financing students during their studies.

Again, young couples often find that, in addition to carrying a mortgage, they are required to take on a great deal of debt to set up house. The burden of this debt may play a major role in family decisions about child-bearing and child-rearing, with some children being brought up in an atmosphere of continual worry about finance. It could be said that these decisions are matters of personal choice and that people must always be left with a clear sense of personal responsibility. However, there must also be a recognition of the pressures under which people are placed, both to consume more and to borrow in order to finance consumption.

To see ourselves . . .

In 1980 the level of personal borrowing in the UK, excluding mortgages, was £11 billion. Today it is in excess of £44 billion. In the area of credit cards and store cards the market has not yet peaked, and could easily double before saturation point is reached. The nature of credit is changing, but there has never been a time when credit was so readily available as it is now. That the use of consumer credit is especially prevalent in the UK is indicated by the following statistics:

Country	Number of credit cards per 1,000 households
UK	1,100
Spain	550
France	400
Germany	75

Recent developments

The change in the nature of consumer credit since the days of "hire-purchase" has been marked, both in the ways in which people borrow money and in the purposes for which they borrow it. Traditionally, hire-purchase was used for the acquisition of consumer durables such as motor cars, televisions, washing machines, *etc.* Today this situation still exists but there is a growing volume of borrowing for current consumption, such as for holidays and fashion items. In such cases the goods or services purchased are often consumed long before the final payment is made.

The nature of credit itself has also changed. Lenders are in the business of lending money and it is in their interests to continue lending to good borrowers, *ie* to those who make regular payments. In this way the volume of credit is maintained. Lenders are continually in search of new borrowers. In such a situation there needs to be continual vigilance to ensure that those most at risk in society are not subjected to unfair pressure to take on more credit than they can manage.

The dangers that lurk

It is easy to assume that credit will solve all your problems. While credit can be a good thing, however there are problems it cannot solve but only make worse.

The usual reasons cited for getting into difficulties with credit are "loss of job", "family/marital problems" and "illness". Lower income families and the young are most vulnerable. They are the ones who are most likely to have to pay the highest price for credit. Some stores charge as much as 40% per annum, while the rate for traders' cheques is about 60%. These rates seem usurious, but of course the rates charged by "back street" money lenders are well in excess of these figures.

It seems apparent that the Consumer Credit Act does not provide sufficient protection for some people. As the Consumers Association comments: "Quite often the APR [Annual Percentage Rate] does not include all compulsory charges. For example now that some credit card companies charge an annual fee to holders, whether they use them or not, this charge does not appear as part of the APR." This might also apply to fees charged for other types of borrowing, *eg* overdrafts.

There is also concern over the liberalisation of consumer credit provision, which has increased the range of providers and allowed onto the scene a number of operators whose disclosure about themselves is inadequate and whose sales practices are questionable. Many of these lend on security of property which is forfeited if the loan is not repaid. And there also seems to remain space within the market for illicit money lenders who charge extortionate rates of interest and employ the most dubious debt-recovery practices.

Sources of credit

As has already been said, the number of purveyors of credit has risen in recent years. This in itself is part of the problem. Credit is available not only from banks, but from retail stores, hire-purchase companies, building societies and, of course, independent money lenders. Many feel that the situation is getting out of control. The *Sun* newspaper's "Money Shop" gives a page listing independent money lenders — all registered under the Consumer Credit Act — but mainly operating as brokers, *ie* using other people's money and sometimes using a car telephone as a point of contact. There seems to be a need for a serious government enquiry to cover the whole issue, especially such matters as the further protection of borrowers and the responsibilities of lenders.

The problem of inducements

A consultant to our group wrote: "People are deluged with vulgar and irresponsible inducements to borrow above their means."

The Consumers' Association reports:

> Sales techniques used by loan providers are often of
> questionable judgement. Lenders might argue that
> credit is just a commodity like any other and that sales
> techniques should reflect this. Yet there are few other
> commodities which imperil people's property in the way
> that some types of consumer credit can do. Free gifts
> and other types of inducement seem calculated to
> overcome the consumer's judgement.

The Church of Scotland Report to the General Assembly
of 1988 on the Ethics of Investment and Banking was
unequivocal on this point: "free gifts", "special offers" and
"instant credit" should be prohibited!

We believe there is a strong case for action to restrain the
more extreme cases of "vulgar inducement" and at least to
demand a more visible "health warning". And it should be
clear that accusations of irresponsibility are not limited to
the "new boys" in the credit scene. Banks and building
societies come in for their share of criticism too.

But perhaps the problem lies in the whole philosophy of
our society today. People get caught in the hype about
consumer goods — which are presented as essentials for
good living — and so are led into debt trying to attain the
life-style which consumerism is meant to yield. In the end
there needs to be a change in the goals and philosophy both
of individuals and of society as a whole.

Usury

The Church's attitude to lending and borrowing has been
heavily influenced by the Old Testament teaching on usury.
To take interest on a loan was forbidden to a Jew in relation
to another Jew, but permitted in relation to a foreigner:
"You shall not lend on interest to your brother, interest on
money, interest on victuals, interest on anything that is lent
for interest. To a foreigner you may lend on interest, but
to your brother you may not lend on interest" (Deut.
23:19–20). The context of this prohibition, namely that of
the small farmer and the moneylender, is important. The
farmer is subject to periodic misfortunes. After a bad
harvest, he may need a loan if he is to survive through

the winter, buy seed and hope for a better harvest next year.

In the New Testament there is no specific guidance on usury, but there is no indication that Christians considered themselves freed from this particular aspect of Jewish Law. The saying of Jesus, "Give to everyone who begs of you and of him who takes away your goods do not ask them again" (Luke 6:30), implies a boundless and reckless generosity in giving, which is beyond the scope of any legislation.

The medieval condemnation of usury was based on the Old Testament condemnation of it, on considerations of Christian charity to the poor and on the need to curb avarice. However, the development of trade in Europe and (after the new discoveries) beyond Europe, meant that enterprises required capital for investment. There was a difference between the peasant farmer needing to buy seed to sow in his fields and the merchant sending his ships on long, risky, but potentially profitable enterprises. This was the new situation (which developed long before the Reformation) to which the old blanket prohibitions could no longer apply, and which they could not and did not control.

Jews were allowed to provide financial services which were forbidden to Christians ("to a foreigner you may lend on interest"). Thus arose the paradox of the Jew, in whose religion the prohibition of usury originated, becoming the usurer and banker of Europe, since his religion did permit him to take interest from Christians.

The Reformed Churches were not bound, as the Church of Rome was, by the old Canon Law. Nevertheless, they had difficulty breaking with the old tradition and in the late 16th and early 17th centuries there was considerable controversy. In 1616 the Scottish divine James Spottiswoode maintained that usury was legitimate under the following circumstances:

- If no advantage was taken of the poor
- If it was practised in accordance with the Christian virtues of amity, equity and mercy
- If it exacted no more reward than the agreed interest rate
- If it accorded with Civil Law.

From that time onwards the balance of opinion tended to rest on the side of a cautious acceptance of usury. Interest rates were fixed (5% being considered reasonable) and the concern of Christian thinkers in the Reformed tradition continued to be the discouragement of avarice and the protection of the poor.

The effect of this biblical testimony seems to be to place moral responsibility on the shoulders of the lender as well as on the borrower — and this would seem to be of increasing significance in a society which has accepted credit as part of its normal life-style.

Covetousness

Another biblical theme which relates to obtaining credit and which is clearly supported in Jesus' teaching is the warning about covetousness. Here, the moral responsibility lies primarily with the borrower. Covetousness is the subject of the Tenth Commandment, but it appears regularly in the New Testament both in Jesus' teaching and in lists of prohibitions in the Epistles. In the Gospel of Luke we find: "Take heed and beware of covetousness, for a man's life consisteth not in the abundance of things he posseseth" (12:15). Jesus clearly stressed individual responsibility with regard to covetousness: "Out of the heart . . . proceedeth covetousness" (Mark 7:21–22). Covetousness is not a superficial thing you can get rid of by rules. It demands a change of heart. But in a society in which economic health rests on maintaining demand, it is easy to drift into a programme of "induced covetousness", with aggressive marketing and demand creation. As the public are bombarded by efforts to persuade them to covet what is on offer, little attention is paid to the virtue of contentment.

It has to be recognised, of course, that the whole economic fabric of our society is at stake here and should not be recklessly disturbed without an appreciation of the consequences. A sudden lowering of the amount of credit in use could result in the reduction of demand for goods and services. And the result of this might well be a growth in unemployment. And yet it must be said that such dependence on credit and on demand creation provides an uncertain foundation for the economic life of a nation — apart altogether from the false hope it breeds in individual citizens.

In this connection it is worth noting the point made by Sir Kenneth Alexander in a letter to the Group:

. . . An increase in saving which was part of a cycle of saving for consumption could actually increase living standards and the demand for and the production of goods and services. The syphoning off of high interest payments from real consumption transfers purchasing power from people with high marginal propensities to consume to people and institutions with a much lower propensity to consume.

What can be done?

(1) Christians believe that part of what it is to be human is to have freedom to exercise *choice* and that this must be maintained in the matter of credit. This means that whatever controls or regulations society imposes we must recognise that the individual adult is responsible for his or her actions. That having been said, however, society has a responsibility to help individuals in the exercise of choice. Education must play a key role in this regard. It is as important to show people how to *use* money as it is to show them how to *make* it. And alongside the need for education is the *philosophical/spiritual* task already referred to, the task of challenging the prevailing spirit of consumerism and of pointing to something better which is worth striving for.

(2) In practical terms, improved credit scoring is clearly required. Banks are doing something about this, but a central register seems to be required. Banks operate a black list on those who are bad credit risks. But is this enough? Is more general information not required if good lending decisions are to be made?

Lenders will usually check with a credit reference agency before making a loan. Information held by these agencies will indicate any previous difficulty which the borrower has experienced. This raises the issue of confidentiality and privacy. Some commentators, including the Consumers' Association and the writers of the Jack Committee Report on Banking Services' Law 1989, believe that this type of information should not be made available to lenders. The lenders themselves — or some of them — would like to go further and have access to information about people who are likely to be good borrowers ("white" information as well as "black" information). The recommendations of the Jack Committee do not favour this development and take the view that there are already too many occasions on which customer confidentiality can be breached. But some improvement in its methods of credit scoring is surely needed.

(3)   One way to combat the over-dependence on credit is to emphasise the benefits of saving. There is no express commendation of saving in the Bible, but thrift and Christian discipleship have often gone hand-in-hand, especially since the economic developments of the 18th century.

Savings banks were started by a Church of Scotland minister who saw the importance of helping poor people to save small amounts which existing banks were not interested in. Saving encouraged an attitude of stewardship which went far beyond the money saved: "saving for a rainy day" became a worthy policy for a responsible person who didn't want to be a burden on others.

There is a strong case to be made for efforts to develop and encourage saving in society in general. If we have the interests of future generations at heart, we must surely find it more important to emphasise savings rather than credit, and thereby build up the nation's resources. It must therefore be a matter for regret that the ethos of traditional savings organisations like the TSB seems to be changing from saving to lending. The sad fact is that in our present-day society credit is much more strongly marketed than saving.

The growth of the Credit Union movement, which encourages savings as a foundation for obtaining credit, deserves support and a lot more encouragement from the mainstream banking sector (see Appendix 6).

In stressing the importance of saving it is important that we do not play down the usefulness of credit — or indeed, ignore the dangers of saving becoming an obsession by which riches are accorded a place they are not meant to have in life. There is a difference between a saver and a miser. A saver is a good steward of his money. A miser loves money for its own sake. The danger from a personal point of view is that we get hooked onto savings in such a way that they become an end in themselves.

As in many other areas of financial activity, so also in credit; proper management is a question of balance. Credit can be (and often is) a financial service which genuinely assists the enrichment of human life. But credit can also be an addiction and people need to be protected from ruthless pushers who are sometimes to be found in sheep's clothing! In a society where making money out of money has become an acceptable form of employment, we have to take a grip on credit before it gets a grip on us. In the present situation there are too many avoidable casualties.

4

The Market

The Village Market

Ever since men moved on from primitive barter, one of the features of civilised life has been the Market. The marketplace was often the place which gave a village its identity and status as a community. It was a facility for the people of a region through which those who had things to sell and those who wanted to buy were brought together for mutual benefit. It was a place where buyers had more choice than they would have had if they had only been bartering with a single producer. In the market, buyers could compare quality, price, delivery *etc*, and get the best bargain. It was also a place where sellers could gauge the needs of potential buyers and subsequently concentrate on producing to meet these needs so that they could be sure of a sale. It was a place where sellers would compete with each other to produce the highest quality at the lowest price to satisfy the customer, and where they would be unable to sell if their price or quality was much inferior to that of other sellers in the market. There was a discipline about the market — but only if there was more than one seller and more than one buyer. If one person controlled all the production of a certain article he could choose his own price, especially if it were a necessary item for life. Such a situation really meant that there was no market and resulted in injustice as people were asked to pay exorbitant prices.

The market, however, was about more than goods and prices and hard business. It was a community event, a place of meeting and friendship, a place of fun for children, a place of opportunity for rogues and twisters. The business and the human element were not kept separate, but were fully intertwined. The market was about buying from someone you knew and could trust, rather than from the person whose price was lowest. It was about maintaining reputations and recognising mutual interest. It was about giving a break to those who had fallen on hard times — the widow and the fatherless — even though their price was not the lowest. Although there is always a danger that we might take a romantic view of the past and ignore its darker side, there is no doubt that the village market was a service to the community at every level.

The market town

When we move from the village market to the market town, we begin to move away from small, personal transactions based on long-standing relationships of trust, to larger gatherings which required more organisation and regulation. The object of this regulation was to uphold fair play and to protect honest sellers and genuine buyers from the activities of those who for their own ends would seek to "distort" the market.

All the market "disciplines" applied here also. But even in the larger market of a town, personal considerations counted for much. Both buyers and sellers would seek the security of long-standing relationships and knew the importance of a reputation for fair dealing. In the more impersonal climate of the larger town, however, there was more scope for the unscrupulous and therefore more need for regulation. But this was always directed towards keeping the market as open and free as possible for the sake of the honest traders.

Principal features

The market in village or town clearly served the needs of the people. The question for us today is whether the vast markets of today — especially the financial markets which are global in character — still serve the interests and needs of people. Before addressing this question, we might review the principal features of the original markets, as follows:

- The people who came to buy and sell were there out of *self-interest* in Adam Smith's sense, *ie* because they wanted to sell something to make money or because they wanted to buy something at as low a price as possible.

- They also came because it was in their *mutual interest* to do so. It was a means of providing a greater *choice* both for the buyer and for the seller in satisfying human needs.
- *Competition* was an obvious element in the market as producers vied with each other to produce goods of the highest quality at the lowest price.
- Allied to competition was the element of *risk-taking* which was required of those who would operate in the market. There was always the possibility that one might commit resources to a product or an enterprise that subsequently failed and thus be left worse off than before. The *rewards* were only there for people who were prepared to take the risks inherent in market operations. (This is a point which those who are involved in the markets today feel is not appreciated by their critics.)
- The market provided a *discipline* for traders. If a seller couldn't move his goods at the price at which he was offering them because others were selling equivalent goods at a lower price, he had to look again at his production methods and profit expectations. The law of supply and demand operated in the market and prices were determined by the balance between the two.

Non-financial forces

Non-financial forces also operated in the market: loyalty, trust, compassion, and so on. Indeed, ever since King Solomon entered into a trading deal with the King of Tyre and found that it created a real friendship between them, commercial relationships have not only been supported by personal considerations, but have instigated personal relationships and enhanced human life. Of course, friendship can also result in blindness to dishonest transactions.

Looked at from the Christian point of view these elements in market life are not unacceptable and in some cases are particularly laudable. There wouldn't be any such facility as the market if people didn't feel it was useful for their lives. They participate in the market because they are accepting responsibility for their own lives and the lives of their families. But they also have a mutual interest in maintaining a fair market. A good market requires a lot of co-operation and trust among traders.

Competition

The idea of competition is sometimes questioned by Christians as a motivation in life and contrasted with co-operation. In a sense, competition is built into the structure of life. If we come to the market with goods or services for sale we hope that others will recognise that ours are among the best available. We work to improve or perfect what we have to offer. We won't be in business for long if we don't. This doesn't mean that there should be no bounds to competition or that Christians approve of those who will grab as much as possible for themselves regardless of others. Competition whose aim is to destroy the opposition in order to create a monopoly is neither fair nor equitable and is destructive of human community.

Christians will always be defining and re-defining "fair competition", but one would expect it to include such things as not deliberately trying to put others out of business; "leaving something on the table for others"; being honest in advertising and sales practices; and getting together with others in the same field to work out common standards and codes of behaviour.

The exercise of competition means that there will be losers as well as winners, and while this is true in many walks of life, Christians can never walk away and ignore their neighbours who have suffered serious misfortune through the operation of market forces. It is this recognition that markets are about people and not just about goods and money which will characterise a Christian's stance in an increasingly anonymous world which too easily forgets the personal.

Need for regulation

Finally, just because Christians are realistic about the nature of man and his propensity to selfishness and sin, they will be concerned that markets are regulated in a way which protects both honest traders and the community at large from those who seek to use the market unfairly for their own ends. Christians, of all people, know that you cannot make men good by legislation and that, indeed, legal constraints by themselves will ultimately not be effective. It is always better to encourage high standards of behaviour rather than have endless laws which invariably can be circumvented. But if the market is to serve the interests of the community, then the community must see to it that it cannot be used merely to satisfy the whims of the powerful. And that requires structures which demand better behaviour and within which those who would do good are not thwarted by the unscrupulous, unregulated behaviour of others.

Important differences

The financial markets of today grew up around the great centres of trade where there was a need for loans, bills of exchange, transfers of money, insurance cover and other financial services. Today they are global in character and even in the last decade have developed at breath-taking speed. In some important respects they differ from the village market. They are not about buying and selling produce, but about buying and selling a share in the owner-ship and profits of a firm. The interest of the shareholder is not in the *use* of the product, either to consume it or to make it into something else. It is in the return on his investment, either through dividends or an increase in capital value. The shareholder is also concerned with obtaining rights of ownership. In buying shares he is not merely buying goods; he is buying the right to determine (with others) the policy of the firm and therefore also the livelihood of the people who work in it.

There should therefore be a different "feel" about the market in stocks and shares. The shareholder cannot just walk away with his purchase and use it as he pleases. He has bought himself into a relationship with a living community of people who to a greater or lesser degree depend on his decisions. He has therefore accepted an awesome responsibility: he is his "brother's keeper".

Impersonal relationships

It is this responsibility which throws into relief the other significant difference between the financial markets of today and the village market of the past. Only a small number of individual people buy shares in firms for themselves. Mostly, shares are bought or sold on behalf of individuals by large institutions, investment trusts, pension funds, unit trusts, insurance companies, banks, and so on. Thus the person who provides the money for the purchase of shares, and who ultimately has a stake in the ownership of a firm, finds himself at one remove from the actual decisions which shareholders have to make. So the markets of today are much more impersonal than their predecessors. Add to this the fact that through modern technology the market has become international and continuous, with people sitting in their offices (or in their homes) with their computer screens giving them all they need to know — while the Stock Exchange building in the City of London is almost deserted. Again, the result is that business becomes even more impersonal than it was with the limited personal contact that was possible on the floor of the Exchange.

The positive

On the other hand, we should not lose sight of the positive side of all this. Through his chosen investment trust, insurance company or pension fund, the individual investor has also taken part in financial provision for a wealth-producing organisation and helped to supply employment for others. Through the market he has an opportunity to take part in the industrial and economic development of his country and of the world and through the wealth generated by his firm's activity to provide (through taxes) the finance which can be used to build schools, hospitals, houses and, in general, to enhance the standard of living of his fellow citizens.

It has to be said, of course, that the average investor does not approach the stock-market with such altruistic intentions. At best, he is seeking a fair return on his capital. But the claim of pro-marketeers is that this has beneficial results not only for the investor but for society as a whole: witness the different levels of living standards in countries with market economies compared with those who have state-controlled economies. South Korea, Taiwan and Singapore are the Third World countries which have embraced the market system, and their performance far outstrips that of countries which have shunned the hard discipline of the market.

Those who commend the market most strongly claim that

it recognises self-interest as a fact of life and seeks to use it for the common good. They also argue that the market system encourages a more efficient use of the earth's resources.

- It instils discipline into economic activity and encourages enterprise.
- It provides the best way for money to be found for all sorts of worthwhile enterprises.
- It demonstrably has raised the standard of living of the ordinary people in the countries in which it operates.
- It is the economic system which recognises more "signals" regarding consumer desires and efficiency of production, than any other system that has been tried.

The negative

On the other hand the market is criticised (even by those who acknowledge that it has an important place in economic life) on the following grounds:

- It is easy to forget and ignore the human effects of the market's activities.
- Decisions are taken only in the financial interests of the shareholders.
- The market favours the strong, the able and the clever over against the weak, the vulnerable and the less able.
- Its interest is often in short-term gains which may not be in the long-term interest of the company or the community.
- It tends to divide industrial enterprises rather than unite them (shareholder interest versus employee interest).
- It cannot deal with environmental problems or with the exhaustion of resources.
- It depends on a continuing philosophy of consumerism which shades into greed.

This last objection has implications for the wider society. In each society a structure of incentives is established (either officially or unofficially) which brings out certain qualities in the people of that society. British society of the 1980s has undoubtedly been affected by the wider application of market forces.

Relevant questions

It is not for the Church to endorse any one economic system. Rather, its task is to scrutinise all systems to see how they match up to its view of God's will for mankind and for the world we inhabit. More especially, it is the task of the Church to challenge the idolatry which would give absolute authority to any man-made system, whether it be capitalist or socialist, free-market or state controlled. Its duty is to remind people that the market is not a self-contained system and that its significance is given to it by that which is beyond it.

One of the first questions to be asked, therefore, is: "Whom does the market serve?" In whose interest does it operate, and who (if any) are its victims? As has already been said, the material standard of living of ordinary people in countries where a market system operates is significantly higher than that in countries where there has been state control. The benefits are there for all to see and many countries which have tried a state-controlled economy have recognised the advantages of the market system and are attempting to adjust their economies accordingly.

But although the market in general has clearly been beneficial, there have also been victims of its functioning. We hear it said: Unfortunately there will be a rise in the numbers of unemployed, but this is the price that has to be paid for getting inflation down. It is not a price which is being paid by everybody. It is being paid by the minority whose lives are disrupted so that the rest of us can enjoy the benefits of a market economy. However necessary it may be to maintain the operation of market forces to the fullest extent possible, it is also important to remember that the market does not operate in isolation from the society which it is meant to serve. It shares the imperfections of that society and the need for modification and regulation in the interests of all its members. We must therefore be on our guard to see that structures which are meant to serve humanity are not given such absolute authority as would allow them to legitimise injustice or ignore human suffering.

Jesus came amongst us "taking the form of a slave", seeing the world from the point of view of one of its victims and becoming a victim himself — the victim of both religious and secular powers. However much we recognise the benefits of the market, we must always scrutinise it from the point of view of the victims of its operation. What we say must express our human solidarity with them.

Concentration of power

Another feature of the market which requires eternal vigilance is the tendency towards concentration of power in the hands of the few. It was because Adam Smith saw this danger that he called on governments to intervene to uphold a truly free market. In biblical times the same problem was faced in a primitive agricultural society. Land was capital and the danger was that, because of one misfortune or another, ownership of land would become concentrated in a few hands and give such landowners tremendous power over the lives of their fellow Jews. For this reason the law of jubilee (similar to the English law of leasehold) was promulgated, whereby all land was to be returned to its original owners every 50 years. Although the law was never fully enforced, it shows the depth of concern there was at the injustices which could follow such concentrations of power.

The present Monopolies and Mergers Commission has done something to redress the balance here, but the threat of the over-concentration of power remains. No system can prevent individuals making the amassing of riches their principal aim in life. But any democratic community must protect its citizens from the oppression which so often follows such ambition.

The ecological issue

One of the most frequent criticisms of the market is that it is too short-term in outlook. One currently relevant mark of this is its inability to take the ecological consequences of its activities into consideration. As Nobel Prize winner Leontief said at the Adam Smith Bicentenary Conference in Edinburgh in 1990: "There are externalities which the market cannot cope with. We live in a different world from Adam Smith." The fear is that the prevailing attitudes in the financial world today encourage aggressiveness towards that world: not co-operation with (*ie* stewardship), but exploitation of the world. The Jews took a long-term view of their use of the land God had given them. They legislated for it to lie fallow every seven years. The rights of ownership were restricted to this extent and those who wanted to exploit earth to the limit were curtailed.

There is enough evidence of the ravages, resource exhaustion and pollution which have resulted from the unrestricted operation of market forces in our day for there to be general agreement that good stewardship of the earth requires an equally determined curtailment of the activities of those who would ruin our heritage for the sake of short-term gain.

Self-interest

In this context the words of a recent vice-chairman of the Conservative Party, are relevant: "We have released the spirit of self-interest but have not disallowed sheer selfishness". It is important to distinguish between the two. There is a strong "communitarian" context for Adam Smith's commendation of self-interest. He assumed the bounds of the nation-state and insisted that the pursuit of self-interested objectives is only tolerable within a framework which reflects man's capacity for fellow-feeling (Appendix 1). For him, self-interest entailed "the natural effort of every individual to better his own condition" and was not to be confused with the activities of "prodigals and projectors". He believed in the need for government intervention to prevent groups of entrepreneurs rigging the market through monopolies, cartels and other means for their own selfish ends and to the detriment of others. This need is as great today. Unbridled self-interest is ultimately a destructive force and its effect needs to be tempered both by legal constraints and by the promotion of a climate of honesty, integrity and concern for one's neighbour.

Mutual interest

Perhaps much confusion has resulted from over-emphasis on the operation of one of the forces in markets, namely that of self-interest, to the virtual exclusion of the other equally important force, namely mutual interest. Without denying the former, it would seem that Christian influence today needs to be given to asserting the importance of the latter: of seeing that the market serves the wider interests of the companies with which it deals and the community in which it is set. It was against this background of *mutual* interest that Adam Smith saw the legitimacy of *self*-interest.

Having said that, however, it must not be forgotten that the essence of the market's success depends on the operation of supply and demand with as little intervention as possible. Where these natural forces are not recognised and are denied expression, they emerge in other forms (*eg* the black market in Eastern Europe). Moreover, the longer these forces are denied, the greater the turmoil and pain that will result when they are finally allowed to operate again. There is a price to be paid for ignoring them.

Striking the balance

It would seem, therefore, that in order for the market to operate for the common benefit of the community, intervention and regulation are necessary. They are necessary, on the one hand, to preserve a "level playing field" and allow the market to fulfil its useful function, and, on the other, to prevent the destructive elements which can easily be released to the detriment of innocent people. (And this must refer not only to the citizens of our country, but especially to those of the "Third World".)

As has been said already, the danger of seeing all economic life in terms of the market is that this tends to narrow the vision and concentrate the mind on figures and finance to the exclusion of people. At its worst this leads to a feeling that people need to be made to fit in to the needs of the market rather than to a perception of the market as essentially a service to people. We need to develop an image of the market in its proper place as part of the whole human enterprise, given freedom precisely for its service to the community of which it is part.

The market is an important human institution. It is regrettable that its development in recent years has been almost entirely in terms of its own interests. The Christian Church, with its infinitely wider concern, needs to play a part in a reorientation of the market's overall aims and objectives.

5

The Market-place
and the Responsible Investor

Capital as a moral instrument

It is said that many of the Christian entrepreneurs in the 19th century recognised three uses for the wealth generated by their business. First, for personal use and the maintenance of a comfortable but unostentatious life-style for themselves and their family. Second, for the expansion of their existing business or the setting-up of new enterprises which would bring jobs and prosperity to the community. Third, for works of charity, either by direct gifts or by setting up trusts for longer-term support for the needy.

They clearly believed that money should be used rather than hoarded (*cf* Jesus' parable of the man who could only think of building bigger barns to store his wealth — Luke 12:18). And in this they were following Calvin, who is reported to have said: "Only money left in a box is sterile. Money used for productive purposes is fruitful." But how can Christians today use their capital as a moral instrument?

The options open to Christians for the use of their surplus finance are many and varied and it should not be assumed that the only option is to store it away in a safe investment. Apart from straightforward support for charitable works and good causes, there is a range of community enterprise trusts, worker co-operatives, third world development trusts and so forth, none of which promise even average annual returns. All of these, however, attempt to use capital invested in a responsible way to bring employment and an enhanced quality of life to those at present excluded from the prosperity of the rest of the world.

In addition, there has been a growth of "Ethical Investment Funds" (see Appendix 5) over the last decade, suggesting that an increasing number of people are concerned not only to get the highest return possible, but to see their capital as a moral instrument used for purposes of which they approve

— and *not* used for purposes of which they disapprove. The weakness of such "Ethical Trusts" so far is that they tend to stress a negative ethical stance — rejecting investment in activities such as gambling, products such as alcohol, tobacco and armaments, or places such as South Africa — rather than positively identifying areas of industry and commerce which should be supported by investment. This can mean that such trusts end up supporting, for example, property investment companies which are not excluded by their own ethical definitions, but which may be involved in dubious dealings which are hardly in line with the moral stance of the investor. Also, by definition, their title tends to imply that traditional investment funds are not ethical, or at least not to the same extent. This is hardly fair, but reflects perhaps an underlying concern with the state of the investment markets.

The other danger is that in concentrating on "ethical" trusts investors feel that they have fulfilled their moral responsibility for the use of their capital. In fact, a far greater responsibility lies upon every shareholder in playing his part in determining the objectives, policies and practices of the companies in which his capital is being used. That duty cannot be wholly delegated to managers of investment funds. Or, if it must be, surely some effort must go into researching the policy and practice of the managers on ethical issues.

Institutionalisation

Since the end of the Second World War an increasing and now dominant proportion of investors' savings has been fed into the market through pension schemes, insurance companies and unit trusts. In 1957, institutional ownership of UK ordinary shares was 21% as compared to 66% by private investors. By 1988 the institutions held 62% of UK ordinary shares, with private investment falling to 19%. The two categories of institution which grew the most were pension schemes and insurance companies, going from 3% and 9% to 29% and 24% respectively over the period (UBS Philips and Drew). Many of the types of institution which now dominate financial markets originated in Scotland, including mutual insurance companies, investment trusts and trustee savings banks.

The benefits of institutionalisation are manifold. A large insurance company, for instance, aggregates and concentrates the savings of many thousands of small investors, reducing their average costs of investment and providing substantial funds for economic expansion and growth. With a few notable exceptions, institutions have proved to be safe and secure havens for people's money. Many people's financial security has been enhanced through their participation in company pension schemes or by the purchase of an endowment policy. In this respect, institutions do a good job. Wealth and the benefits which flow from them have been spread widely throughout the population by the advance of these savings media since the war.

Yet many investors in insurance products or participants in a pension scheme are unaware that the premiums they pay are invested in companies listed on equity markets. They believe they are merely "buying an endowment policy" or "contributing to the pension scheme". The institution stands between them and the market to the extent that it obscures from the investor's sight the companies into which the savings are invested. Thus the investor has no direct link to the assets in which his savings are invested. The capital for which he is responsible is out of his control.

The practicalities of seeking to influence a large institutional investor are daunting. If I am one of the many policy holders of a large mutual insurance company, how can I influence it on investment matters, far less a large public company in which the insurance company holds, say, less than 1% of the issued capital?

This is one of the major drawbacks in the institutionalisation of savings. British company law gives the shareholder a voice in the company's affairs through his right to attend, speak and vote at general meetings of the company. But the power to exercise that right is concentrated in the hands of large institutions. Most institutions are run by serious and honest people whose prime concern is and has to be the financial security of and returns achieved for their investors. But this can lead to an over-concentration upon the solely financial aspects of being a "responsible investor" and draw attention away from other aspects of corporate activity.

It would, of course, be quite wrong to imply that private investors acting on their own will be either more or less greedy or prudent than institutions. But by acting through institutions they are handing over to others a responsibility which is their own for the welfare of the companies in which their money is invested.

Ethical issues raised by market-place institutionalisation

Some of the ethical issues in the market-place are no different from those which apply to any other area of human life. People should not steal or defraud. They should speak the truth and honour their promises. These are straight-forward matters. The reaction to the sentences given following the Guinness trial confirms that people expect to see criminals brought to book. (Certain directors of Guinness were convicted of fraud in connection with the takeover of Distillers Company Limited.)

The problems of an institutionalised market for savings are less obvious. By investing through an institution the individual *divorces the benefits of investments from the responsibilities* that apply to holding shares in a company. Policyholders in Standard Life, for example, are not invited to the Annual General Meetings (AGMs) of the companies in which their premiums have been invested. Indeed, few institutions even bother to send a representative to such meetings. Thus, institutionalisation tends to produce *passivity* in all respects other than financial returns.

The responsibility for the day-to-day running of a company lies with its board and management. On the most important issues of corporate management, shareholders are able to vote at the AGM. It is extremely rare for institutional investors to force change upon a company's management. Even more so is it rare for them to ask their own investors' views on anything.

By delegating authority over his money to an insurance company or unit trust, the individual excludes himself from decisions such as takeovers, mergers, acquisitions and so on. It is quite possible that someone working for, say, an engineering firm and having an insurance policy with a major life company could find that a successful takeover bid for his employer had hinged upon his insurer selling a large stake in his employer, which as a result had left him out of a job.

Too often, markets measure success only in numerical terms, partly because there are so few other reliable indicators. But the investor may have an agenda different from that of the institution, one that includes items other than financial return only. The institutionalised market-place finds it hard to hear these voices, so preoccupied is it with the noise of the numbers. Very often, institutional shareholders are really trading investors rather than partners in an enterprise, thereby accepting the responsibilities which go with share ownership. The holders of the share capital of a company are not the only group with a legitimate interest in the way it is run. Yet the ultimate decisions are theirs.

An agenda for improvement — a published mission statement

Is there any way by which shareholders' concerns can be fed into the corporate thinking of an institution? In his book *Moral Man and Immoral Society* (Faber & Faber 1948), the theologian Reinhold Niebuhr has maintained that "individual men . . . may be able to consider interests other than their own . . . but this is more difficult if not impossible for human societies and groups." The group exists for the benefit of its members, and its officers believe it to be their responsibility to defend and advance the interests of the members at all costs. This often leads to rigidity of thinking and to more "unrestrained egoism than the individuals who compose the group reveal in their personal relationships." There seems, therefore, to be a need for some mechanism by which wider concerns of ethically motivated shareholders can be incorporated into the stated aims of the firm.

One way forward would be for investment institutions to be *required* to produce a "mission statement" setting out their objectives as a firm together with the principles governing the way they do business. This would enable all concerned to see the standards the organisation has set itself and to judge its performance accordingly.

Mission statements would enable the investor to know more about their activities on a broader range of issues than merely the generation of investment returns. A mission statement would cover the following:

- financial goals, in terms of potential returns and attitude towards risk
- policies towards employees
- attitude towards takeovers and mergers

- policy towards companies in which the assets are invested, (attendance at AGMs, non-executive directors *etc*)
- average expected duration of investments (short-term or long-term)
- code of conduct of employees.

(The existence of such a statement on behalf of financial institutions could have a distinct effect on companies hoping for investment finance.)

The mission statement would be published in all the company's literature, available to all potential investors. There could also be a useful improvement in corporate financial reporting to cover areas other than those which receive most attention at present. Not least of these would be a requirement for boards to provide an annual assessment of how the company has done against the standards set for itself in the mission statement. This would enable the investor to see not only their performance record (always superb!) but to assess how they have gone about achieving it as well.

What would this achieve? By telling investors (and others) the attitude of the board of the company toward a wide range of issues, opportunities for constructive dialogue would be opened up. It would be possible to judge the progress of an institution on a wider range of criteria than merely financial returns.

For investors, the mission statement would improve and inform choice. Company A offers a unit trust which makes all its money out of "playing" potential takeover targets and has a great long-term record, growing by 15% on average over the past ten years. Company B offers a fund with a similar but slightly inferior record, having grown by 13% on average, yet has a consistent record of being a dedicated long-term investor. Today, the potential investor would know little of the two alternatives beyond their records. If their investment style was accessible through a mission statement, then the investor's choice would be rather better informed. Many people might prefer Company B. The choice — properly informed — should be theirs.

Such mission statements may not immediately change investment practice all that much, but at least they would put the ball back in the investor's court. Investment need not be a blind search for the highest returns, but a choice among competing institutions who disclose fully their philosophy and practice.

New wine in old wineskins?

There is much that can be done within the present financial structures to encourage responsible institutional share ownership. But do the structures themselves still support and assist that objective? It would be surprising if legislation originally introduced to fit the situation of the mid 19th century still fully met the needs of today despite the numerous Companies Acts in the intervening period.

There is no question that the key to much of the economic expansion of the last century or so has been the passing of the Companies Act of 1862 permitting the creation of the joint stock company with limited liability for shareholders. The previous forms of industrial co-operation through family businesses and partnerships had meant that all of a person's assets could be called on to pay for debts incurred by the firm. The limitation of liability made possible a great increase in the amount of capital available for expansion — something which family firms and partnerships could never have achieved. Initially, within the limited liability company, the idea of partnership remained strong among investors. The shareholders were usually few in number and known to one another, and had some sense of being trustees for the human and material organisation which was their firm. They were well aware of the need for profit, and sought it for themselves. But their interest in the firm was wider and more long-term in nature.

As trade expanded and shares became more widely traded, however, the owners of shares in a firm became less and less known to each other. Their interest was focused more and more on the financial return the company might be expected to provide.

This process gathered speed with the growth of stock exchanges and took a decisive step forward with the development of institutions which provided a professional service for the management of the investor's financial assets. This too, as has been said, was of undoubted benefit to shareholders.

But conditions have changed radically from the 1860s, and some of the developments resulting from the Act providing for limited liability were not foreseen and were surely not intended. The Act referred to a situation where the majority of shareholders were private investors. It assumed that such shareholders would have an interest in the character of the firm, in its products or services, in its reputation and long-term welfare and in the human community which constituted it. Of course, the investor was interested in the firm's profit and in his share of it. But here again he was more likely to be interested in dividends (which entailed a long-term interest) rather than in capital gain (which so often leads to short-term thinking).

Today's shareholders, whether individuals or institutions, are constrained by the conditions in which they operate to be interested almost entirely in the firm as a vehicle for financial return. And yet shareholders retain the rights they held in 1862 as full partners in an economic enterprise.

There is a growing sense of unease about this situation in many quarters of the business world today. *The Economist* has recently described shareholders today as mere "punters" who speculate on companies in the same way as race-goers bet on horses (and no one would dream of giving the punter even a share in the management of a horse!). There will always be people — perhaps the majority — who want to use the market only in this way. But should they be accorded the rights of ownership if they are unwilling to accept its responsibilities? An absentee shareholder is no better than an absentee landlord.

The health of a company depends on having owners who have a real concern for its long-term success and welfare. As it has turned out, however, control of many firms is ultimately in the hands of those who have only a speculative interest in the company. If capital is to be used as a moral instrument, then we need structures which will place ownership and control in the hands of those who have the long-term interests of the business at heart.

It is not our function to say what new structures are appropriate, though the Church played a leading role in raising public consciousness of the need for change after the disastrous failure of the City of Glasgow Bank in the last century. So today the Church's task is to voice a concern that present structures no longer fit the conditions of financial practice and positively discourage the efforts of those who want to see a more responsible deployment of their capital.

Various efforts have been made to fashion new structures alongside the present ones. Names like "John Lewis Partnership", "Scott Bader", "National Freight" and "Sears Roebuck" come to mind. Common to all seems to be the idea that the destiny of a company should be in the hands of *trustees* who see the future growth and well-being of the company — and the human community it represents — as their first concern. Such an idea accords well with the idea of stewardship and with a recovery of some sense of partnership among the various groups — including finance — which have an interest in the destiny of the firm.

The danger of seeking a blueprint for universal application must be stressed, however. There is much need for learning from what is already happening, recognising underlying principles, and introducing structures which will encourage and serve the needs of our day.

6

Christians in the Financial World Today

The Christian's dilemma

As has already been said, we are living in a dynamic society in which the pace of change seems to quicken decade by decade, if not year by year. Unless one chooses to withdraw from the world to a life of seclusion, it is impossible not to be affected by the changes which have occurred over the last decade or so, some of which are for the better and some, regrettably, for the worse.

Over the past few years, with disconcerting suddenness advances in telecommunications have shrunk the many markets of the world into one single market. In the UK, where both London and Edinburgh perform important functions within the market, we have experienced substantial upheavals through the internationalisation of the markets ("Big Bang"), self-regulation and de-regulation. During that same period we have witnessed scandals in the City where previously there had been trust underscored by the ethic of "my word is my bond".

Many Christians are employed in the financial markets; upon these individuals many others depend for financial security through pensions, insurance and prudent investment of savings. The world of finance is one whose spirit and practice can often be at odds with Christian teaching; it is therefore to be expected that Christians will be faced with situations which would seem to challenge their personal standards. The very fact that money is the basic commodity being dealt with inevitably increases the intensity of the ethical issues which have to be faced. The basic problem for Christians is that of being "in the world but not of it".

Those working in the financial sector are not unique in facing these difficulties. Many in the arms, tobacco, advertising, drugs and alcohol industries may often have to wrestle with their consciences — as do their colleagues in medicine, law and the ministry. But in the financial world this conflict is more obvious.

> Even where there is no deliberate intention to break the law or sail close to the wind, the pressure of increased competition, the presence of many grey areas, the need to hold down a job and the obligation to work with and for others with different standards, all combine to create an environment in which it is not always simple for Christians to be clear about their duty — or even when they are clear, easy to do their duty. (Commission Report, Church of Scotland)

Over-judgemental?

Sometimes the Church seems over-judgemental in its attitude to those of its membership who work in the financial sector. Perhaps what these individuals most need is support and understanding. The plea has been presented by one of them in these terms: "We need some kind of vision which will allow us to operate in this vital area of human life, to be at ease with ourselves and to get rid of the feeling of guilt." It is also maintained that it is only when you have felt the anxieties connected with working in the financial world that you are able to comment on its ethics with real understanding.

One thing is clear, however: Christians should not opt out from business and finance. Jesus did not withdraw his disciples from the world and protect them from the temptations of the day. He sent them out into the world. And as he sent them he sends us. Our problem is how to be involved in the world of finance with its inevitable compromises and grey areas, while remaining true witnesses to our Christian faith.

Even among Christians there will be differences of opinion as to what that "true witness" is. Perceptions of truth have changed over the years in the light of the changed circumstances of human life. In confronting these differences we must be sensitive to others' points of view, respecting them (while not necessarily accepting them), maintaining what we believe to be right and continuing to love those with whom we disagree. Professor Ronald Preston writes:

Most areas of ethical decision are ambiguous. Thus if we can arrive at some broad consensus on the direction we want to go, a kind of middle ground, we will achieve a lot in helping Christians to form opinions ... Listening to one another within the body of Christ is a salutary exercise, even if we have to go on living together with disagreements in ethics as we do in doctrine. (*Finance and Ethics*, Centre for Theology and Public Issues, 1987)

A vast market

The financial world today covers not only the traditional areas of banking, insurance and stock markets, but has extended to include relatively new financial instruments such as financial and commodity futures, interest and currency hedges and oil swaps. Each traditional market has exposures within itself and new "products" are continually being introduced to the markets. Many, it has to be said, emanate from a marketing sales base rather than a traditional financial base. It is a vast market which has a momentum of its own and many feel relatively powerless within it.

But it is not only the products and size of the market which have changed over the years. The standards within the industry have changed too. Sometimes what was the norm (or even the common exception) has become not only frowned upon but made illegal by legislation (*eg* trading in securities with the benefit of privileged information). In this respect standards may be said to have been raised. But on the other hand there are signs of a decline in standards which give cause for increasing concern. A senior investment manager of a Scottish insurance company has said: "There is no question but that the system of trust which existed when I became involved in the business has deteriorated remarkably over the past decade."

As these deficiences in the market have been increasingly publicised, other pressures have been brought to bear on both the market and the government for there to be a clearly defined set of rules both for the players and their clients. The Financial Services Act 1986 has been enacted and self-regulation under the Securities & Investment Board (SIB) and its various bodies has followed. It is within all this turmoil of change and opportunity that Christians have to work out their ethical stance. They may also need to argue for the worth of high ethical standards in a world where that is not always accepted.

The nature of man

One of the fundamental contributions which Christians bring to the consideration of the ethical problems of the financial world is a realistic assessment of the nature of man. "Man is very far gone from original righteousness," say the Thirty-nine Articles. This sounds grim and discouraging. But it is only on the basis of a realistic picture of human nature that we will discover an ethical foundation for life in the financial world of our day. There is a false idealism around (in both capitalism and socialism) which pretends that people can be depended upon to act from altruistic motives. We need to be continually challenging this secular optimism about man with Christian realism about his true nature. The structures and practices which we fashion must take account of human selfishness. They will succeed only if this basic reality is recognised. It was because Jesus knew what "was in man" and faced it realistically, that he was able to offer an ethical stance which enshrined both justice and compassion. It is on this basis that we approach the ethical problems of the financial world.

A different song?

The most notable contribution of a Christian in the financial world is not a collection of do's and don'ts, but the fact that he comes with a "different song". He exudes a spirit which rises above secular individualism and tells of a better life than this world by itself can ever give. It is always the call to the Christian in the world "to sing the Lord's song in a strange land" (Psalm 137:4).

Ethics in a pluralist society

Christians do not bring something obscure or other-worldly to the human scene. They come believing that the teaching of Jesus is for the financial world too. Jesus was not talking about something labelled "religion", but about human life in all its aspects. We assume — as he did — that there is something in every man which is able to recognise and respond to the Gospel.

It is therefore important to see that ethical issues are raised and discussed openly in the belief that others will recognise truth even though no religious language is used.

The basis of such dialogue must be: (1) an acknowledgement that Christians have no monopoly of the truth and (2) a genuine effort to listen to what others are saying in the hope of discovering truth together.

Co-operation with other Christians

Christians in the financial world, as elsewhere, need the support of fellow Christians. We can't walk alone. Since the calling of the Twelve by Jesus, discipleship has never been individualistic. Christians need one another to share thoughts, ideas, concerns and strategies, and to give more publicity and weight to their efforts. Since the passing of a predominantly rural society, Christians have never discovered how to get together with fellow Christians who share a similar experience in working life. Ways need to be found for Christians in the financial world to get together without setting themselves apart from the rest of their working colleagues.

Revolution or evolution?

There is a natural caution among Christians about advocating revolutionary change in society. So often the consequences of such changes have not been fully foreseen. "Looking for revolutionary change is a temptation rather than a vocation!" said one of our members. There is a prophetic strain in the Bible which calls for drastic change in the name of justice. And it could be argued that revolution has taken place — and needed to take place — in Eastern Europe today. But unless such change is part of a larger process of evolution and transformation, it inevitably leads to further problems. Jesus is certainly looking for a transformation of human life, but he seems to have rejected the ways of the revolutionaries of his day. He calls us to be salt and yeast and light in the world: Christians are to add savour, transform and bring illumination to the human situation.

The dilemma of the agent

When a Christian is employed in the financial service industry, he is usually operating as an agent rather than as a principal, and his freedom of action is subject to the constraints imposed by that role. He cannot act on his own behalf and may find himself prevented from doing what he believes ought to be done (see Appendix 2). This is not a new situation for Christians to find themselves in, but it can raise ethical issues which are not easily decided. It is in relation to such situations that the support of, and dialogue with, fellow Christians is most needed.

Ways of coping with the role of agent might include:

- Without being aggressive about it, making sure that it is widely known that you are a Christian. It will then not come as a shock either to the principal or to colleagues that you should take a certain ethical stance.
- In cases of uncertainty (grey areas) the agent may feel that he has a responsibility to fulfil the instructions of the principal to the best of his ability, but in so doing may seek opportunities of accentuating that which is good and wholesome.
- In the course of his work the agent can be on the look out for opportunities to mention ethical problems and possibilities — in carefully controlled "doses" — as a consciousness-raising exercise, pointing to values which should be considered.
- In discussion with principals a Christian may feel able to introduce wider issues and mention social ends as well as financial returns.

A caring society

Although it may not be in their main line of business, it may not be unimportant for Christians to try to involve employers and others in charitable causes. Should not mission statements speak of involvement in the local community and in family care, or declare support for the One

Per Cent Club? (The One Per Cent Club is a group of firms who promise to devote 'one per cent of their profits to charitable causes.) Such information would be important to investors, depositors and employees. Raising awareness in such ways would not only benefit the community, but also keep the need for social responsibility on the agenda of the firm or the institution.

What do Christians bring to the scene?

(1)   *A life-style* which does not allow wealth or riches to cut them off from others and which more positively breaks down social barriers by knowing and moving among ordinary people. Should not Christian bankers know more about credit unions and give them a hand? Could not investment managers help with community enterprise in its efforts to raise funds and use them wisely? Such action would give a new dimension and meaning to the words "financial service".

(2)   *An attitude to money* which doesn't see the making of money as the most important objective in life, but which paradoxically brings a refreshing freedom from concern about money. It is an attitude which includes scrupulous honesty, of course, but is also concerned with broad fairness, *ie* with not taking advantage of the weak and the vulnerable. It involves obeying the spirit of the law with a streak of generosity wherever possible: *eg* "always leaving something on the table for someone else" and not being "so greedy that you want to squeeze every last penny from a deal" (*cf* the biblical admonition to leave the gleanings in your field for the poor and the stranger in Deuteronomy 24:21).

(3)   *An awareness of the personal dimension of every transaction.* This entails drawing attention to those who will be affected by decisions and actions and stressing that financial actions are not, humanly speaking, neutral.

(4)   *An attitude to wealth in terms of stewardship.* This has been argued elsewhere. It is an attitude which challenges the idea that our ownership is absolute and that we can do what we like with what is ours. Rather, it acknowledges that "The earth is the Lord's and the fulness thereof" (Psalm 24) and that we are trustees entrusted by God with some part of his creation. His offer to us is to enjoy the use of it, but also "to tend and to keep it" for him. To see wealth in terms of

stewardship means accepting gratefully the gift: not being afraid of it but not allowing the spirit of greed to take over; taking care in our use of it that it may bear good fruit for ourselves and for others; and using it in such a way that will leave the world a richer place because of our trusteeship.

(5) *A critical function.* A Christian's witness will always include a readiness to recognise weaknesses and injustices in present structures and practices and the courage to point these out and discuss them with others. Working for change in structures and practices is slow and demands painstaking effort, but it is part of the Christian contribution to the life of any sector of society, not excluding the financial sector.

(6) *A method of working through institutions.* Christians should be alive to the positive possibilities of compromise in working through institutions. Compromise may mean not getting all that one wants, but recognising what is worthwhile in what has been agreed, stressing these gains and supporting them as a step towards something better. Christians also have the task in institutions of reminding people of the highest objectives of the organisation, defining them and re-defining them in terms of the present situation.

(7) *Church action.* There may also be a place for Christians through their Churches to pressure financial institutions to maintain high standards of personal conduct and to lobby the government to encourage savings. The Church, as a sort of ethical guardian, might even convene groups to give people the opportunity to scrutinise mission statements and company reports.

Professional spirit

Every profession is concerned about ethics today. It became clear to our group that people are saying: "We need a new spirit in our profession". It is up to Christians to point to the source of that new spirit.

In talking of the Kingdom of God, Jesus was describing among other things a community of trust. This is the foundation of Christian ethics. The best conditions for trust exist when people belong to a small community and have known each other over a period of time. Although these conditions are experienced less and less in today's market conditions, the Scottish financial community is small enough for there to be much scope for the exercise and promotion of trust. One of the tasks of Christians operating within this community is to strengthen the spirit of trust and to commend its importance and worth to their colleagues.

Appendix 1: Adam Smith: Ethics and Self-interest

Notes from a paper given to the Working Group on Finance and Ethics by Prof. Andrew Skinner, FRSE, of Glasgow University

Historical context

Smith is talking in terms of a particular historical situation — the breakdown of the feudal state and the growth of commerce. In this new situation all goods and services command a price, thus eliminating the "bonds of dependence" (as in the feudal state). The Sovereign, therefore, no longer needs to superintend the industry of private people; thus, in Smith's view, the objective should be to reduce constraints on people and allow growth. "The natural effort of every individual to better his own condition ... is so powerful a principle that it is alone ... not only capable of carrying on the society to wealth and greatness but of surmounting a hundred impermeant obstructions. ...."

Moral dimension

The call for individual liberty, Smith argues, must be seen within the context of some accepted code of behaviour. Smith says that man is possessed of "fellow-feeling": "However selfish man may be supposed, there are evidently some principles in his nature which interest him in the fortunes of others." Moreover, "Nature, when she formed man for society, endowed him with an original desire to please, and an original aversion to offend his brethren." Smith also maintains that, "Without regard to general rules of behaviour, there is no man whose conduct can be depended upon."

The conscience of society

Smith insists that the pursuit of self-interested objectives is tolerable only within a framework which reflects man's capacity for fellow-feeling. He suggests that the conscience of society will disapprove of unfair play because of its "fellow-feeling with those who suffer the consequences".

But Smith notes, as Prof. Skinner explains, that "where men act with an eye to the positive rules of moral conduct — where behaviour is marked by beneficience with regard to other (which is perfectly consistent with the pursuit of the objectives of self-interest) — then that society 'flourishes and is happy'. If, on the other hand, justice alone is the rule, then life in society may be characterised by nothing more than 'a mercenary exchange of good offices according to an agreed valuation'".

Appendix 2: Wealth and Riches — Ethics and Morality: Two Important Distinctions

Robin Angus

"Yes — but what do you actually mean by . . .?"

If one is putting forward a case for a set of beliefs, it is important that the language in which this is done is intelligible. "Dialogue of the deaf" is a theological "buzz-phrase" much in use these days, and for good reason. Not all speech or writing is communication! For this reason, I should like to make clear my personal understanding of two distinctions which, I believe, are important to the work of the group. It is true that these have been touched upon in several places in this book. But I believe them to be so essential to our task that I would like to repeat them here.

Distinguishing "wealth" from "riches"

The first of these is the distinction between *wealth* and *riches*. These words are often used as synonyms. As I myself prefer to use them, they are opposites. It is impossible to arrive at a balanced understanding of the relationship between Christianity, economics and personal morality unless one distinguishes clearly, as I believe the Bible does, between *the amassing of riches* (which is essentially sterile and selfish, and which the Bible condemns) and *the creation of wealth* (which is a model and mirror of God's creation, and which the Bible holds out to us as an example).

Chapter 2 rightly points out that the Bible is full of ideas and images of "abundance", "increase", "plenteousness" *etc*, and makes the necessary point that Jesus was himself a wealth creator in the truest sense when he worked as a carpenter: he took raw materials and, through his time and skill, made them into implements for everyday use. It is too often wrongly supposed that "wealth" means only "great wealth", rather than the fruits of the labour of an individual or of a small group.

All Christians are called upon to be creators of wealth. When we create something good or useful, we are in a sense sharing in God's eternal and never-ending act of Creation. The factory worker making a car, the miner digging coal, the parent cooking a meal for the children are all "wealth creators", just as much as the industrialist whose capital funds the factory or the mine, or who sells the ingredients for, or pays the parent who cooks, the family meal.

But the Bible explicitly condemns the amassing of riches in bigger and bigger barns. When I say that examples of the *amassing* as opposed to the *creation* of wealth might be the anti-social stockpiling of cars or coal to create a shortage and hence an artificial and inflated profit, or the hiding of piles of black-market tins in the larder during a period of rationing, the distinction I see between the two will, I hope, be clear. But too often the right use of God's creation (the creation of wealth, for the benefit of others as well as for one's own benefit) is confused with the selfish keeping to oneself of its fruits (the amassing of riches).

Distinguishing "morality" from "ethics"

The second distinction I wish to draw is between *ethics* and *morality*. Again, as commonly used, these words are treated as synonyms. I prefer to use them, not as opposites, certainly, but as ideas which are complementary to each other. Too often, when we speak of a business being run "ethically", we mean only that it is run in accordance with the letter and the spirit of the law, and in full accordance with (say) the rules of the stock exchange or some other professional code of practice.

It is, of course, right and proper that businesses should be run in this way. But it is not enough. Obeying the law is of itself no more praiseworthy than observing the highway code or the rules of golf or the rules of a social club, which is what one should be able to take for granted among motorists or golfers or club members.

To me, running a business "morally" should be something more than just sticking to the rules (that is, running it "ethically"): it should be the deliberate *cultivation of the good*, not just the *avoidance of the bad*. For this reason, I like to draw a distinction between "ethics" (which nowadays tends to mean, in business, just adhering carefully and exactly to the rules and to the principles of professional "best practice"), and "morality", which I see as something wider and more fundamental. (My *Pocket Lexicon* tells me that "ωos", as used in the New Testament, just means "custom" or "rule", as in Luke 1:9, "κατὰ τν ωos της ιερατειας", "according to the custom of the priesthood", so perhaps I am justified in making the distinction I do between "ethics" and "morality"!)

Our group should not primarily be concerned with the "ethics" of business in the sense in which I have just used the word. We must *begin* where "ethics" (in this sense) *ends*, by trying to discover how Christians can add something in the financial world over and above what is (rightly) required by the law or by the various professional associations.

The agent's dilemma

By and large, those not active in the financial world would be amazed by how strictly honest and "ethical" it is. Laws are certainly broken and corners are cut by a tiny few, but, in my experience, standards of obedience to the law and to the various professional codes are much higher than many outsiders suppose. The main problem is that financial practitioners have much responsibility but little power.

This is because financial practitioners are usually *agents*, not *principals* — in other words, they are stewards of other people's money, not their own. Their freedom of action is therefore limited. I have the right to invest my own money as I please, to further my own causes and beliefs. I do not have the right so to invest the money of other people, who may not share these causes and beliefs or may even be actively opposed to them. This is a point of critical importance, because it is often supposed by outsiders that it is the financial practitioners who ought to be persuaded into supporting, say, Scottish industry or community-based projects with the money they manage. But this misses the point. Even if they *could* be so persuaded, they would not have the *right* to do it. It is not *their* money, any more than the funds of a congregation are the personal property of the minister, to be disposed of as the minister wishes!

Well-meaning people who urge insurance or pension fund managers, or other financial practitioners, to back this or that admittedly praiseworthy use of resources with the funds they manage are therefore not just wasting their time. They are actually urging financial practitioners to do what would be *selfish and wrong* — namely, to pursue their own causes at other people's expense.

Instead, the way forward is to heighten the consciousness of the *owners* of the money which the investment managers manage (the pension fund beneficiaries, the people who hold insurance policies or save in banks or building societies or hold investment trust shares or unit trust units) and educate *them* in the rights and responsibilities which they as capital owners (and someone with £100 in a building society is a capital owner just as is a millionaire financier) ought to exercise. It is thoroughly frustrating for financial practitioners to hear people complain that they are evading their responsibilities, when in fact the people complaining do not realise that they are the ones who actually employ the financial practitioners as their agents through their membership of pension funds or through holding life assurance policies!

The need for patience and urgency

This change will not be achieved within the lifetimes of any of us. It calls for a fundamental change in society: the stitching back together of the rights and responsibilities involved in capital ownership, which became detached in most people's understanding when investment became institutionalised earlier in this century. Chapter 3 appropriately highlights the Reformation emphasis on individual responsibility as against the pre-Reformation Church's emphasis on the collective social responsibility of humankind. But the truth is, of course, that both are right, but that each is incomplete without the other. Moreover, while Christians must be content to work gradually to change the thinking of society, they must also work at this task diligently and with urgency; the fact that we know that change must be gradual should not make us lazy or pessimistic about trying to promote it.

It is a paradox of Christianity that Christians must work hard and urgently for results which they know may be slow in coming and which they themselves may never see. Jesus apparently had very little to show for his intense and exhausting earthly ministry, but in that ministry he began the process which has changed and is still changing the world. We must have both Jesus' urgency and Jesus' patience in co-operating with him in the stewardship of God's creation and in trying to create a society which understands what wealth is and what capital is and how capital should be rightly used and wealth rightly created. We need to cultivate in society a *financial* moral sense which will shape the use of capital in the future, and this will take not years but generations to achieve.

This, however, must not discourage us or make us look for a quick and easy solution. Such a solution does not exist. It is always easy to turn things upside down and to destroy: it is much harder to change and to build. So we must begin with ourselves, in accordance with the Protestant insight, *and* co-operate with others with the aim of gradually changing society, which, in turn, will have the power gradually to change *us*, in accordance with the Catholic insight.

For this process to begin, it is of vital importance that financial practitioners, professional theologians and the users of financial services (the people in the pew, who may not see themselves in this way) all co-operate with and educate one another. A society in which the wealth of creation is used rightly in the creation of wealth for all cannot possibly come about through the actions of financial practitioners alone. Nor can it come about through the efforts of professional theologians alone, or of the users of financial services alone. But if all of us talk to one another, co-operate with one another and teach and educate one another in a continuing and open process, then at least a start can be made.

Appendix 3: Is there a Duty of Self-fulfilment?

The Very Revd Prof. James A. Whyte

One of our Consultants, commenting on our draft report, said: "Self-discipline, self-responsibility, is easier if we don't have any hang-ups about self-fulfilment." And he added that there is a *duty* of self-fulfilment.

Christianity appears to be hostile to the idea of self-fulfilment. The saying of Jesus, "If any man will come after me, let him deny himself and take up his cross and follow me," suggests that self-abnegation rather than self-fulfilment is the aim and character of the Christian life. But the saying which follows closely on is: "For whoever would save his life shall lose it, and whoever loses his life for my sake will find it." Is there a hint here that what is offered is not the way of self-destruction, but the true way of self-fulfilment? Self-concern is self-defeating. The deeply selfish person destroys himself — and many others besides. The one who gives himself in the cause of Christ — the reference is clearly to martyrdom — finds true self-fulfilment.

Self-denial as preached and practised in some Christian circles has often seemed to proceed from fear and hatred of self, from a putting-down of the self. When asked what such extremes of self-denial and mortification were in aid of, the ascetic could only answer, "To make me holy." Such self-denial is a form of self-creation, and is therefore ultimately self-centred — and it is not simply the softness and self-indulgence of our day that finds it unattractive.

On the other hand, the commonest idea of self-fulfilment appears to be in terms of the Porsche and the Mercedes — success as measured by possessions. A good deal of self-denial, in terms of lost sleep and long working hours, may go into the acquisition of these possessions, yet few would argue that this is the self-denial of which Jesus is speaking. Here the New Testament gives a firm reminder that a man's life does not consist in the multitude of things he possesses.

Similarly, people may deny and discipline themselves in the quest for the perfect physical form, spending much time, effort and money on diets, exercises and treatments. This is a form of self-fulfilment, but hardly the most lofty.

Humanistic psychologies in the United States make "self-actualisation", the full development of one's potential, an aim in life. This seems much worthier than a materialist idea of self-fulfilment, but it is still a self-regarding activity, and it takes no account of our infinite capacity for self-deception. (Which is one of the things that Christian teaching means by "original sin".)

It may be that Christian self-denial is neither self-hatred, self-contempt nor self-love, but is rather self-forgetfulness, the forgetfulness of self that comes when one is concerned for the other rather than oneself. Self-denial is thus an aspect of love.

The insistence that Christians must deny themselves for the sake of the poor, and must defend the poor and the dispossessed and the powerless of the earth, would seem to be in line with this concept of self-denial. This is a proper expression of self-denial in the modern world: self-denial for the sake of justice, expressing God's concern for all who are weak and defenceless.

The question must then be asked: Do Christians have no concern for the rich, the successful and the powerful of the earth? It is to this group, relatively speaking, that most of us middle-class, professional Westerners belong. Is energy, enterprise and self-forgetful dedication Christian only when it is on behalf of the needy, seeking a fairer distribution of wealth? Is it not Christian when it is seeking (in the sense that we have defined in Chapter 2) the creation of wealth? It would be unfortunate if the Christian passion for the first were not balanced by an understanding of the importance of the second.

Many Christians, and others, have found that the way of self-denial that entails loving dedication to others — within the family, or in charitable or caring work — is in fact the way of self-fulfilment. The Christian paradox is true: "For whoever would save his life shall lose it, and whoever loses his life for my sake shall find it." But we have limited this view to the charitable and caring professions, giving the impression that in these only is there a Christian vocation. Can the truth of the Christian paradox be found by those who are working in industry and in the financial world?

It is not difficult to see Christ in the poor, so that what is done for them is "for his sake". It is not easy to see Christ in firms or financial institutions. Indeed, there has always been a danger that we give unstinted service and unselfish loyalty to institutions and groups that are themselves entirely selfish and careless of the needs of others. A purely personal morality, of unselfishness and service, is not enough. There must be a morality of the institution: what ends does it serve, and by what means are these ends achieved?

Such critical thought is required equally in charitable enterprise. If it is wrong to do evil that good may come, it may be even more blameworthy to do good that evil may come — that is, to engage in misguided charity that makes the situation worse rather than better. The major charities, such as Christian Aid and Oxfam, are well aware that "aid" may in the long run be harmful, and that the concept of "development" requires careful and critical thought.

So the distinction between charitable and financial enterprise may not be so great as at first appears. Both demand critical thought about the morality of institutions, and about the likely consequences for the human enterprise of the actions that are being taken. Both operate in circumstances where the choice is often to seek the lesser of two evils. In both, as in all other human enterprises, we are liable to self-deception, thinking of ourselves as nobler than we really are. But in both it may be possible for those who forget themselves to find true self-fulfilment.

Appendix 4: Bank Secrecy and Money Laundering

Dr Charles W Munn

There have recently been a number of well-publicised cases of abuse of the international banking system. In some cases the abuse has become institutionalised. This can happen where secrecy is a commodity for which financial institutions charge a price. In these cases secrecy can be maintained even against the government and other authorities of the country in which the bank is situated. This facility is open to abuse. Banks and other financial institutions may accept deposits and provide other services to people with something to hide — usually the profits from illegal activities. In this way the banking system becomes involved with the criminal fraternity and is therefore seen in the same light. Countries such as the Cayman Islands have laws which are extremely difficult to penetrate. In other places, such as Switzerland, which have a reputation for maintaining secrecy, the laws have become less stringent in recent years. Nevertheless, Swiss banking laws still afford much greater possibilities for concealment than the laws of other countries. There is a wider problem at issue here inasmuch as Companies Acts in many countries enable the ownership of registered companies, not just banks, to be kept secret. It is difficult to escape the conclusion that people who seek secrecy have something to hide. The recent case of the Bank of Credit and Commerce International is a case in point. This organisation used its domicile in several countries to construct a complex web of deceit and criminality.

Perhaps even more worrying than the institutionalised version of this problem is the fact that the problem can arise without anyone being aware of it. This can happen when bankers unwittingly accept deposits which are the product of criminal activities. It must be said here that it is well-nigh impossible for a banker to be aware of the sources of all of his customers' deposits. Recent guidelines issued by the Bank for International Settlements, endorsed by the Bank of England, which give advice to bankers on how to deal with this problem are welcome. The basic advice is that bankers should get to know their customers better. This is sensible, but it remains to be seen just how practical it is. Furthermore, in the money laundering process, funds are usually moved several times. How is a banker to know, on the second or any subsequent move, that the funds in question are of dubious origin?

It seems unlikely that the guidelines already issued will be sufficient in themselves to provide a solution to this very worrying problem. In 1991 the British Bankers' Association, in association with the Building Societies Association, the National Drugs Intelligence Unit, HM Customs and Excise and the Police produced a booklet for the guidance of bank staff on how to deal with the problem of money laundering. A number of banks are following this up with instructional material for staff which will educate them in how to recognise the tell-tale signs of abuse of the banking system. These are important steps forward, but the point is made that this guidance is made for "all mainstream banking and deposit taking financial institutions within the jurisdiction of the United Kingdom".

In dealing with this difficult problem, the banks have to tread a fine line between the public obligation to expose suspected criminal activity and the obligation to their customers to maintain confidentiality. This was a point stressed in the recent Jack Committee Report on banking law. There is an important distinction to be made here between the concepts of confidentiality and secrecy. Confidentiality is the obligation to customers not to reveal information about their affairs to people who do not have a right to that information. Secrecy, on the other hand, involves the payment of a price for the service of protecting information about investments against all third parties.

There is every sign that British banks are acutely aware of the danger of being sucked into the trap of money laundering and that they are making strenuous efforts to avoid doing so. This might also be said of other countries, most notably France. However, until the problem is tackled on an international basis and strenuous efforts are made to put pressure on countries which make a virtue of their secrecy laws, the problem will not disappear. There are many signs that the international banking community will be galvanised into action by the BCCI scandal. The problem of money laundering can only be tackled on an international basis. It is in the banking community's own best interests to address the problem vigorously and promptly. Without this action the reputation of the whole banking system may be tarnished.

Appendix 5: Ethical Investment: How it arose and how it is developing

George Harte

How it arose

One of the earliest indications of ethical investment since the industrial revolution and the development of the capitalist market economy was the investment policy of some American religious institutions, who in the 1920s removed investments in "sin stocks" (alcohol, gambling and tobacco) from their portfolios. However, impetus for recent interest was provided mainly by the Vietnam War and by apartheid in South Africa. In the 1960s and 1970s an anti-war sentiment in the United States encouraged various groups, including religious ones, to challenge the role of the weapons and chemicals manufacturers. For some, one form of action was to disinvest from such companies. In addition, investment funds appeared which pledged not to invest in companies with military links; these were the so-called "peace portfolios". In Britain, the interest was less with the Vietnam War and more with the plight of Black and Coloured South Africans suffering under apartheid. Of particular concern was the extent to which many of the largest British companies were heavily involved in the South African economy.

An important development in Britain was the challenge to Quakers posed by the Young Friends Central Committee in 1980. Their report identified matters beyond the recognised concern with investing in companies involved with armaments, tobacco, alcohol and gambling. It suggested a more fundamental review of Quaker investment policy, and expressed a desire to inform individual Quakers, raising other issues such as the use of power by multinational companies, company advertising, and investment in South Africa. The Young Quakers suggested the need to focus on what could be considered socially useful and socially harmful production. This report was followed up by other publications by the Committee which continued the theme and stressed a new objective for investment, namely the use of capital to promote social good. Perhaps of most importance was the subsequent development of an information and research service and of the first ethical unit trust soon afterwards. In 1983 EIRIS (Ethical Investment Research Services) was formed to provide information for potential ethical investors, both institutional and private. And in 1984 the first ethical unit trust was launched by Friends Provident. Both had direct links to the Quakers.

Following the setting-up of the Friends Provident Stewardship Trust in 1984 a number of other ethical and environmental unit trusts have been established in Britain. These unit trusts are the most visible sign of ethical investment in Britain today. A recent count suggested that there are now 23, although it is important to stress that these unit trusts account for less than £300 million in invested funds and represent less than one per cent of the unit trust market in Britain. They also differ to varying degrees in their emphases, with some stressing the ethical or social dimension while others specialise in environmental matters. In the case of the latter, some (the environmental opportunities trusts) appear to be primarily concerned with investing in companies which seek to achieve financial gain from the current interest in the environment. The following list indicates the variety of concerns covered by the ethical and environmental unit trusts:

- production or sale of alcohol or tobacco
- gambling
- armaments manufacture
- operation in South Africa
- operation in other countries with repressive regimes
- labour relations and conditions at work
- equal opportunities
- training
- environmental impact
- advertising
- involvement in the nuclear industry
- production or sale of sexually explicit or violent magazines or video tapes
- contribution to community welfare
- respect for animals

How it is developing

It is somewhat ironic, though perhaps not surprising because of the nature of our society, that for some people the future of ethical investment depends on whether it is possible to invest and obtain as good financial returns as before. As yet there is limited evidence available, yet the answer could be crucial to the development of ethical and environmental investment by pension funds. It is estimated that approximately $400 billion of funds invested in the United States are socially screened. These are in large part funds of state pension schemes. In Britain, trust law, particularly that governing trustees' duties to beneficiaries, appears to discourage such investment.

Future developments in ethical investment should also be seen in the context of a number of other issues. The concern with business and investment short-termism calls for greater shareholder involvement in the running of companies, and greater discussion of business ethics all suggest that there may be impetus for ethical investment from a number of quarters. Two further influences would appear to be particularly crucial. First, the rise of ethical investment has been followed by an increasing consumer pressure, particularly in relation to environmental impact. There is a marked similarity between the issues focused on by the critical consumer magazines and the issues identified by the ethical unit trusts.

Secondly, and most importantly, the increased awareness of environmental problems has begun to influence all walks of life. Many of the matters referred to, such as business ethics, will have to be reconsidered with a new environmental dimension. Recently, EIRIS announced that it is expanding its collection of information on environmental matters. "Green" issues such as nuclear power, CFCs, pollution, greenhouse gases and waste *etc*, are now high on the ethical agenda. In fact, for many people the two should be seen as one and the same thing. Both investors and consumers can be expected to demand information indicating the full price being paid for their consumption and profit. One important and influential development may be the Valdez Principles, named after the Exxon tanker disaster. These principles have been developed by concerned investor and environmental groups, and are intended as both something companies can become signatories to and a means by which corporate performance can be judged. The ten principles cover matters such as protection of the biosphere, sustainable use of natural resources, reduction and disposal of waste, use of energy, disclosure of incidents and hazards, assessment and annual audit. Such publication of general principles or the development of specific company codes of conduct could increase the discussion of ethical and environmental matters. It may well be that by being accountable for such wider social aspects of performance, companies will hasten the development of ethical and environmental investment.

Appendix 6: Credit Unions

Revd Ian Fraser, Community Minister, Greenock

In one large housing estate on the north side of Edinburgh there is a resident population of about 40,000. But there are no banks — not even a savings bank. People have to travel up to a mile out of their district into one of the more prosperous areas of town to obtain the services of a bank.

But the residents of such areas have begun to form their own organisations for saving and borrowing. These are called credit unions. Credit unions are *financial co-operatives* owned and controlled by their members. They are led by devoted volunteers who put in many hours of unpaid work to set up and maintain local community banks.

Forty such community-based credit unions exist in Strathclyde alone and in addition there are occupational credit unions among bus drivers, train drivers, taxi drivers, police officers, firemen, teachers, social workers and many others.

The aims and objectives of credit unions are:

- To promote systematic saving by encouraging members to save a small amount each week
- To eliminate usury and to increase the purchasing power of members by enabling them to borrow money at low interest rates
- To train and educate members in business methods and self-government, and to help them realise the value of co-operation and mutual support
- To promote democracy by operating through a board of directors, a credit committee and a supervisory committee, elected by and from the members
- To create alternative personal financial services in the community under the ownership and direction of members.

Anyone over 16 can apply to become a member of a credit

union. Once approved, the full member pays an entrance fee (usually £1 or less) and buys a share (usually £1). Each member has one vote, irrespective of his or her savings level, but only members over 18 can apply for loans.

The ultimate control of a credit union lies with the members, who meet once a year in the AGM. But the job of running the union is delegated to a board of directors, elected by the membership at the AGM. Under the board there are two main committees — the credit committee, which considers loan applications, and the supervisory committee, which has specific duties under the law, including checking members' passbooks and preparing bank reconciliations. All officials and members — except the treasurer, who can be paid an honorarium — must serve without pay.

Loans are granted to members who can show they have a need, have a good record of savings and repayment and can prove their ability and intent to pay. The policy of the union is to meet the borrowing requirements of as many members as possible; therefore, small loans will usually be given priority over large ones.

By law, a credit union cannot charge more than 1% per month on the unpaid balance of any loan. This represents a cost of about £6.50 on a loan of £100 repaid in 12 monthly instalments — in other words, an annual percentage rate of about 13%, compared with at least double that from commercial sources and at least five times that from non-institutional sources, such as money lenders (which are on the increase). Interest on loans and investments is used to pay for expenses and to build up reserves, and also to pay small dividends to members.

As well as regularly banking the monies received, the credit union must keep full books of account and produce financial statements. In addition, annual certified accounts must be lodged with the Registrar of Friendly Societies.

With one in every thousand people members of credit unions in mainland Britain, the British movement has some way to go before achieving the success of other credit union movements internationally. In Quebec one in every two people are members and in Ireland one in every four.

Appendix 7: Memorandum submitted to the Independent Inquiry into Corporate Takeovers in the United Kingdom, April 1990

1. *In the first place we would like to say that takeovers of themselves are neither good nor bad.* There are times when a takeover will be of benefit to the community and times when it will do no harm to the community. Also, it is not necessarily the case that too many takeovers are happening at the present time. (Here we would be fully in sympathy with what Sir Gerald Elliot says about the need for re-grouping and responding to changing situations.) What is happening is that there are too many takeovers of the wrong sort.

2. *Our concern* arises *from the following*:

a) *Too many takeovers seem to be founded on a too narrow view of what a company really is.* They are motivated by short-term thinking which sees the company merely as a vehicle for money-making and financial speculation. Such a view disregards the many social and human factors which make up the real ethos of the firm and give it an important place in society. It ignores the commitment of employees to the company and their justified expectation of life-fulfilment for themselves and their families. And it is unheeding with regard to the effects of a takeover on the complex relationships between a firm and its suppliers, its customers and the community in general. The gap between the thinking of the City and that of people in industry is one of the most distressing features of our economic life. Some of us would, indeed, go as far as to say that an almost complete gap has opened up between money and stocks and shares on the one hand, and on the other hand the real wealth in human and productive terms which money, stocks and shares represent.

b) *Further, our concern arises from the fact that the real owners — the shareholders — are largely passive and do not exercise the responsibilities which come with ownership*. This is not so much by design as by the evolution and convenience of financial institutions. But the fact is that in law as in intention they have given instructions to their representatives to the effect that "financial return" is to be the only criterion for managing their funds. And yet as shareholders they have final legal responsibility for the life and destiny of the company and of its employees.

c) *We are concerned about the adverse effect of the threat of a takeover on the performance and decision-making of managements*. This has been well documented elsewhere and we would have little to add to what has already been said by such as Sir Hector Laing. We do recognise, however, the danger of the threat of takeovers leading managements to go for short-term success to the neglect of long-term development.

d) *We are concerned because there seem to be increasing doubts about whether takeovers do in fact lead to a more efficient use of resources*. Facts known to some members of the Group suggest that this is by no means always the case and the extra time spent in re-organisation and personal (as well as personnel) re-adjustment can severely limit the hoped-for increase in efficiency. The fact that Germany and Japan have efficient industries without the trauma of take-over battles suggests that there are other ways of achieving efficiency, and it is no accident that in the case of these two countries the ownership of industry has established itself on co-involved and consultative lines, rather than on the detached and adversarial lines familiar in the UK. In Germany and Japan, as in many other capitalist countries, industry tends to be regarded as an enterprise in which the nation and society share, rather than as a battleground for financiers alone.

e) *We are concerned because too often the motive for a takeover is not the industrial logic of the case but rather the greed, ambition and desire for empire-building on the part of one or more individuals* who enjoy the power game but are heedless of the wider human consequences of their actions. You can't make people good by legislation but the law must protect the community (especially the most vulnerable) from the activities of such people.

f) *Allied to this, we are concerned about the growth of a*

financial services industry which needs "to make things happen" and which exerts a sinister influence by encouraging individuals to make bids from which the brokers and merchant bankers will earn healthy fees. Admittedly, they have an attentive audience but their true "service" should be a different one.

g) *We are concerned because takeovers usually represent a centralisation of power* (although we recognise the good features of the trend towards "unbundling"). A healthy democratic society depends on the dispersal of power and the maintenance of independent centres of economic activity. The danger of centralisation is a vital one for a region or for a nation like Scotland, not least because takeovers often have the effect of draining away talent and removing leadership from a community.

h) *We are concerned because of the abuse of the right to compete in a free society.* Competition is a natural component of a healthy industrial/commercial society. But in some takeover "battles" we see competition run riot. When people begin to use military terms, negotiation and rational debate are usually left far behind. In a well-integrated society there is surely a place for an informed and constructive debate about a company's future, in the course of which due weight is given to the company's business, to the people whom it employs and to its importance in the wider community.

3. *Underlying convictions*

a) *Wealth creation is important for the life and health of a nation and its people.* In this regard we in this country have inherited a strong industrial base which needs to be continually renewed in each generation. We have a responsibility to be good stewards of the real wealth of our nation and its communities. But money creation is not necessarily wealth creation. And where money creation is not related to wealth creation a society is in danger.

b) *Ownership of wealth brings responsibilities which cannot be shrugged off or passed on to someone else.* The danger of our situation is that, in the person of the shareholder, ownership has become separated from responsibility — because of the growth of institutions aimed at making investment simpler and safer. Many of the problems with takeovers stem from this abdication of responsibility by shareholders. (This seems to apply also to their representatives, the fund managers, who often would rather "walk away" from a deteriorating situation than organise a common recovery programme; as would tend to happen, for instance, in other European Community countries.)

c) *There is always a danger in making money the measure of success — or indeed the measure of true wealth.* Wealth in the form of money easily distances a person from the responsibilities which come to the holders of wealth. It is assumed that one has a right to do what one likes with one's own money. And yet this right represents power over people when it is used and therefore carries responsibility.

d) *The issue of takeovers raises a question of simple justice.* It is basically unjust that a company which has taken many years to build up and has given (and continues to give) good service to the community in which it is set and with which it has deep and strong relationships should have its fate sealed in a matter of weeks by a hostile bid which promises short-term gains to institutional shareholders who have no interest in the real purposes of the firm apart from immediate financial return.

4. *Proposals*

a) *Limitations on the rights of short-term or speculative shareholders* such as: withholding voting rights on shares until a year after purchase; allowing differential voting rights on different classes of capital; increasing the Capital Gains Tax burden on shares traded within a year of buying (other than when such shares are forcibly acquired after the success of a bid) *etc.* Such limitations would not diminish the rights of shareholders in general. Indeed, they would increase the rights and influence of long-term shareholders by guarding them against dilution by the actions of short-term speculators.

b) *New mechanisms for helping individual investors to exercise their responsibility as owners.* The first step here should be a campaign by companies, the government and industry as a whole to bridge the "indirect share ownership consciousness gap", whereby most of the many millions of people who own shares through participation in pension scheme, life assurance and other collective savings enterprises simply do not realise that they are shareholders in companies and that, hence, takeovers and takeover policy are matters of direct and immediate consequence to them.

c)   *Changing the remit of fund managers* in two ways: first by mobilising public and industrial opinion to discourage the growing belief that short-term (often quarterly) performance statistics are the measure of such managers' success, rather than a more prudent three or five years; and, second by changing the law (where such changes are required) to allow trustees or directors of pooled funds, and the managers of such pooled funds, to take into account when making investment decisions matters other than immediate, tangible, realised capital gains, without fear of adverse legal consequences to themselves. Trustees, directors and managers all need and deserve what is already possessed by direct individual shareholders: the right to say no to take-overs on moral, ethical, regional, strategic or other broader grounds, not just on short-term quantifiable financial grounds.

d)   *More stringent company law to restrain power-hungry tycoons and the "intermediaries" who aid and abet them.* Should not the costs of the successful defender be borne by the unsuccessful bidder rather than by the defending company's shareholders?

e)   *More stringent rules relating to registration of shares held in nominee names* to make it easier to identify the ultimate beneficial owner.

f)   *A much wider remit for the Office of Fair Trading,* enabling it to take into account issues other than those of the narrowest "anti-competitive" sort.

g)   Proposals for *alternative methods of improving the efficiency of a firm* without a takeover.

h)   *A statement of the criteria for judging a legitimate takeover.* A check-list against which the bidding company would have to justify its case and the defending company would have to answer, might include these questions:

• Does the takeover make industrial logic?

• Would it improve the position of the company?

• Is the "mix" compatible?

• Is the aim to suppress or to expand?

• What will be the effect on the local community?

• Is it an "unbundling" exercise, *etc, etc*?

Note: We believe that none of the proposals here suggested would adversely affect genuine investors in listed companies. Nor would they interfere to any great extent with the free market in company securities. They would prove awkward only for raiders and short-term speculators.